Table of Contents

Introduction

Welcome to the Love Poem Collection, the largest selection of love poems! I carefully picked the greatest love poems from the English literary history so you can enjoy it at the comfort of your home. The book is divided into 6 parts, each dealing with a different aspect of love, from being in love to losing love. Inside each chapter, you can find the love poems and quotes in ascending chronological order. So, at the beginning of the chapters, you will find poems from the 16th, and at the end you will find poems from the early 20th centuries.

George Chityil
Collector

Poems About Being in Love

La Vita Nuova

In that book which is
My memory . . .
On the first page
That is the chapter when
I first met you
Appear the words . . .
Here begins a new life

Dante Alighieri (1265-1321)

To His Love

Come away, come, sweet love,
The golden morning breaks,
All the earth, all the air
Of love and pleasure speaks,
Teach thine arms then to embrace,
And sweet rosy lips to kiss,
And mix our souls in mutual bliss.
Eyes were made for beauty's grace,
Viewing, rueing love's long pain,
Procur'd by beauty's rude disdain.

Come away, come, sweet love,
The golden morning wastes,
While the sun from his sphere
His fiery arrows casts:
Making all the shadows fly,
Playing, staying in the grove,
To entertain the stealth of love,
Thither, sweet love, let us hie,
Flying, dying, in desire,
Wing'd with sweet hopes and heav'nly fire.

Come away, come, sweet love,
Do not in vain adorn
Beauty's grace that should rise
Like to the naked morn:
Lilies on the river's side,
And fair Cyprian flowers new blown,
Desire no beauties but their own,
Ornament is nurse of pride,
Pleasure, measure, love's delight,
Haste then, sweet love, our wished flight.

Anonymous (1500-1600)

Dear, I to thee this diamond commend

Dear, I to thee this diamond commend,
In which a model of thyself I send.
How just unto thy joints this circlet sitteth,
So just thy face and shape my fancy fitteth.
The touch will try this ring of purest gold,
My touch tries thee, as pure though softer mold.
That metal precious is, the stone is true,
As true, and then how much more precious you.
The gem is clear, and hath nor needs no foil,
Thy face, nay more, thy fame is free from soil.
You'll deem this dear, because from me you have it,
I deem your faith more dear, because you gave it.
This pointed diamond cuts glass and steel,
Your love's like force in my firm heart I feel.
But this, as all things else, time wastes with wearing,
Where you my jewels multiply with bearing.

Sir John Harrington (1539-1613)

One day I wrote her name upon the strand

One day I wrote her name upon the strand,
But came the waves and washed it away:
Again I wrote it with a second hand,
But came the tide, and made my pains his prey.
Vain man, said she, that dost in vain assay
A mortal thing so to immortalize!
For I myself shall like to this decay,
And eek my name be wiped out likewise.
Not so (quoth I), let baser things devise
To die in dust, but you shall live by fame:
My verse your virtues rare shall eternize,
And in the heavens write your glorious name;
Where, whenas death shall all the world subdue,
Our love shall live, and later life renew.

Edmund Spenser (1552-1599)

The Nymph's Reply to the Shepherd

If all the world and love were young,
And truth in every shepherd's tongue,
These pretty pleasures might me move
To live with thee and be thy love.

Time drives the flocks from field to fold,
When rivers rage and rocks grow cold,
And Philomel becometh dumb;
The rest complains of cares to come.

The flowers do fade, and wanton fields
To wayward winter reckoning yields;
A honey tongue, a heart of gall,
Is fancy's spring, but sorrow's fall.

Thy gowns, thy shoes, thy beds of roses,
Thy cap, thy kirtle, and thy posies
Soon break, soon wither, soon forgotten,--
In folly ripe, in reason rotten.

Thy belt of straw and ivy buds,
The coral clasps and amber studs,
All these in me no means can move
To come to thee and be thy love.

But could youth last and love still breed,
Had joys no date nor age no need,
Then these delights my mind might move
To live with thee and be thy love.

Sir Walter Raleigh (1552-1618)

from Astrophil and Stella

Queen Virtue's court, which some call Stella's face,
  Prepar'd by Nature's choicest furniture,
  Hath his front built of alabaster pure;
  Gold in the covering of that stately place.

The door by which sometimes comes forth her Grace
  Red porphir is, which lock of pearl makes sure,
Whose porches rich (which name of cheeks endure)
  Marble mix'd red and white do interlace.

The windows now through which this heav'nly guest
  Looks o'er the world, and can find nothing such,
Which dare claim from those lights the name of best,

Of touch they are that without touch doth touch,
  Which Cupid's self from Beauty's mine did draw:
  Of touch they are, and poor I am their straw.

Sir Philip Sidney (1554-1586)

The Bargain

My true love hath my heart, and I have his,
By just exchange one for another given:
I hold his dear, and mine he cannot miss,
There never was a better bargain driven:
My true love hath my heart, and I have his.

His heart in me keeps him and me in one,
My heart in him his thoughts and senses guides:
He loves my heart, for once it was his own,
I cherish his because in me it bides:
My true love hath my heart, and I have his.

Sir Philip Sidney (1554-1586)

Damelus' Song to Diaphenia

Diaphenia, like the daffadowndilly,
White as the sun, fair as the lily,
Heigh ho, how I do love thee!
I do love thee as my lambs
Are belovëd of their dams—
How blest were I if thou wouldst prove me!

Diaphenia, like the spreading roses,
That in thy sweets all sweets incloses,
Fair sweet, how I do love thee!
I do love thee as each flower
Loves the sun's life-giving power,
For, dead, thy breath to life might move me.

Diaphenia, like to all things blessed,
When all thy praises are expressëd,
Dear joy, how I do love thee!
As the birds do love the spring,
Or the bees their careful king,—
Then in requite, sweet virgin, love me!

Henry Constable (1562-1613)

My lady's presence makes the roses red

My lady's presence makes the roses red,
Because to see her lips they blush for shame.
The lily's leaves, for envy, pale became,
And her white hands in them this envy bred.
The marigold the leaves abroad doth spread,
Because the sun's and her power is the same.
The violet of purple colour came.
Dyed in the blood she made my heart to shed.
In brief: all flowers from her their virtue take;
From her sweet breath their sweet smells do proceed;
The living heat which her eyebeams doth make
Warmeth the ground and quickeneth the seed.
The rain, wherewith she watereth the flowers,
Falls from mine eyes, which she dissolves in showers.

Henry Constable (1562-1613)

To His Coy Love

I pray thee, leave, love me no more,
Call home the heart you gave me!
I but in vain that saint adore
That can but will not save me.
These poor half-kisses kill me quite—
Was ever man thus servèd?
Amidst an ocean of delight
For pleasure to be starvèd?

Show me no more those snowy breasts
With azure riverets branchèd,
Where, whilst mine eye with plenty feasts,
Yet is my thirst not stanchèd;
O Tantalus, thy pains ne'er tell!
By me thou art prevented:
'Tis nothing to be plagued in Hell,
But thus in Heaven tormented.

Clip me no more in those dear arms,
Nor thy life's comfort call me,
O these are but too powerful charms,
And do but more enthral me!
But see how patient I am grown
In all this coil about thee:
Come, nice thing, let my heart alone,
I cannot live without thee!

Michael Drayton (1563-1631)

The Passionate Shepherd to His Love

Come live with me and be my love,
And we will all the pleasures prove,
That valleys, groves, hills and fields,
Woods or steepy mountains yields.

And we will sit upon the rocks,
Seeing the shepherds feed their flocks
By shallow rivers, to whose falls
Melodious birds sing madrigals.

And I will make thee beds of roses,
And a thousand fragrant posies,
A cap of flowers and a kirtle
Embroidered all with leaves of myrtle;

A gown made of the finest wool,
Which from our pretty lambs we pull;
Fair-lined slippers for the cold,
With buckles of the purest gold;

A belt of straw and ivy buds,
With coral clasps and amber studs;
And if these pleasures may thee move,
Come live with me and be my love.

The shepherds' swains shall dance and sing
For thy delight each May morning;
If these delights thy mind may move,
Then live with me and be my love.

Christopher Marlowe (1564-1593)

Sonnet 116

Let me not to the marriage of true minds
Admit impediments. Love is not love
Which alters when it alteration finds,
Or bends with the remover to remove:
O no! it is an ever-fixed mark
That looks on tempests and is never shaken;
It is the star to every wandering bark,
Whose worth's unknown, although his height be taken.
Love's not Time's fool, though rosy lips and cheeks
Within his bending sickle's compass come:
Love alters not with his brief hours and weeks,
But bears it out even to the edge of doom.
If this be error and upon me proved,
I never writ, nor no man ever loved

William Shakespeare (1564-1616)

Sonnet 18

Shall I compare thee to a summer's day?
Thou art more lovely and more temperate:
Rough winds do shake the darling buds of May,
And summer's lease hath all too short a date:
Sometime too hot the eye of heaven shines,
And often is his gold complexion dimmed;
And every fair from fair sometime declines,
By chance or nature's changing course untrimmed;
But thy eternal summer shall not fade,
Nor lose possession of that fair thou ow'st;
Nor shall death brag thou wander'st in his shade,
When in eternal lines to time thou grow'st:
So long as men can breathe, or eyes can see,
So long lives this, and this gives life to thee.

William Shakespeare (1564-1616)

Sonnet 130

My mistress' eyes are nothing like the sun;
Coral is far more red than her lips' red;
If snow be white, why then her breasts are dun;
If hairs be wires, black wires grow on her head.
I have seen roses damasked, red and white,
But no such roses see I in her cheeks;
And in some perfumes is there more delight
Than in the breath that from my mistress reeks.
I love to hear her speak, yet well I know
That music hath a far more pleasing sound;
I grant I never saw a goddess go;
My mistress, when she walks, treads on the ground.
And yet, by heaven, I think my love as rare
As any she belied with false compare.

William Shakespeare (1564-1616)

The Passionate Pilgrim

Fair is my love, but not so fair as fickle;
Mild as a dove, but neither true nor trusty;
Brighter than glass, and yet, as glass is, brittle;
Softer than wax, and yet, as iron, rusty:
A lily pale, with damask dye to grace her,
None fairer, nor none falser to deface her.

Her lips to mine how often hath she join'd,
Between each kiss her oaths of true love swearing!
How many tales to please me hath she coin'd,
Dreading my love, the loss thereof still fearing!
Yet in the midst of all her pure protestings,
Her faith, her oaths, her tears, and all were jestings.

She burn'd with love, as straw with fire flameth;
She burn'd out love, as soon as straw outburneth;
She fram'd the love, and yet she foil'd the framing;
She bade love last, and yet she fell a-turning.
Was this a lover, or a lecher whether?
Bad in the best, though excellent in neither.

William Shakespeare (1564-1616)

Cherry-Ripe

There is a garden in her face
Where roses and white lilies blow;
A heavenly paradise is that place,
Wherein all pleasant fruits do flow:
There cherries grow which none may buy
Till 'Cherry-ripe' themselves do cry.

Those cherries fairly do enclose
Of orient pearl a double row,
Which when her lovely laughter shows,
They look like rose-buds fill'd with snow;
Yet them nor peer nor prince can buy
Till 'Cherry-ripe' themselves do cry.

Her eyes like angels watch them still;
Her brows like bended bows do stand,
Threat'ning with piercing frowns to kill
All that attempt with eye or hand
Those sacred cherries to come nigh,
Till 'Cherry-ripe' themselves do cry.

Thomas Campion (1567-1620)

Elizabeth of Bohemia

You meaner beauties of the night,
That poorly satisfy our eyes
More by your number than your light,
You common people of the skies;
What are you when the moon shall rise?

You curious chanters of the wood,
That warble forth Dame Nature's lays,
Thinking your passions understood
By your weak accents; what 's your praise
When Philomel her voice shall raise?

You violets that first appear,
By your pure purple mantles known
Like the proud virgins of the year,
As if the spring were all your own;
What are you when the rose is blown?

So, when my mistress shall be seen
In form and beauty of her mind,
By virtue first, then choice, a Queen,
Tell me, if she were not design'd
Th' eclipse and glory of her kind.

Sir Henry Wotton (1568-1639)

Song: To Celia

Drink to me, only, with thine eyes,
And I will pledge with mine;
Or leave a kisse but in the cup,
And Ile not look for wine.
The thirst, that from the soule doth rise,
Doth aske a drink divine:
But might I of Jove's Nectar sup,
I would not change for thine.
I sent thee, late, a rosie wreath,
Not so much honoring thee,
As giving it a hope, that there
It could not withered be.
But thou thereon did'st onely breathe,
And sent'st it back to mee:
Since when it growes, and smells, I sweare,
Not of it selfe, but thee.

Ben Jonson (1572-1637)

To Celia

Drink to me, only, with thine eyes,
And I will pledge with mine;
Or leave a kiss but in the cup,
And I'll not look for wine.
The thirst that from the soul doth rise,
Doth ask a drink divine:
But might I of Jove's nectar sup,
I would not change for thine.
I sent thee, late, a rosy wreath,
Not so much honouring thee,
As giving it a hope, that there
It could not withered be.
But thou thereon didst only breathe,
And sent'st back to me:
Since when it grows, and smells, I swear,
Not of itself, but thee.

Ben Jonson (1572-1637)

Her Triumph

See the chariot at hand here of Love,
Wherein my lady rideth!
Each that draws is a swan or a dove,
And well the car Love guideth.
As she goes, all hearts do duty
Unto her beauty;
And enamour'd, do wish, so they might
But enjoy such a sight,
That they still were to run by her side,
Through swords, through seas, whither she would ride.

Do but look on her eyes, they do light
All that Love's world compriseth!
Do but look on her hair, it is bright
As Love's star when it riseth!
Do but mark, her forehead's smoother
Than words that soothe her;
And from her arched brows, such a grace
Sheds itself through the face
As alone there triumphs to the life
All the gain, all the good, of the elements' strife.

Have you seen but a bright lily grow,
Before rude hands have touch'd it?
Ha' you mark'd but the fall o' the snow
Before the soil hath smutch'd it?
Ha' you felt the wool o' the beaver?
Or swan's down ever?
Or have smelt o' the bud o' the briar?
Or the nard in the fire?
Or have tasted the bag of the bee?
Oh so white! Oh so soft! Oh so sweet is she!

Ben Jonson (1572-1637)

Love Me Not for Comely Grace

Love me not for comely grace
For my pleasing eye or face,
Nor for any outward part,
No, nor for my constant heart.
For those my fail or turn to ill,
So thou and I shall sever.
Keep therefore a true woman's eye,
And love me still, but know not why;
So hast thou the same reason still
To doat upon me ever.

John Wilbye (1574-1638)

There is a Lady Sweet and Kind

There is a lady sweet and kind,
Was never face so pleas'd my mind;
I did but see her passing by,
And yet I love her till I die.

Her gesture, motion, and her smiles,
Her wit, her voice, my heart beguiles,
Beguiles my heart, I know not why,
And yet I love her till I die.

Her free behaviour, winning looks,
Will make a lawyer burn his books;
I touch'd her not, alas! not I,
And yet I love her till I die.

Had I her fast betwixt mine arms,
Judge you that think such sports were harms,
Were't any harm? no, no, fie, fie,
For I will love her till I die.

Should I remain confined there
So long as Phoebus in his sphere,
I to request, she to deny,
Yet would I love her till I die.

Cupid is winged and doth range,
Her country so my love doth change:
But change she earth, or change she sky,
Yet will I love her till I die.

Thomas Ford (1580-1648)

To Anthea, Who May Command Him Anything

Bid me to live, and I will live
Thy Protestant to be;
Or bid me love, and I will give
A loving heart to thee.

A heart as soft, a heart as kind,
A heart as sound and free,
As in the whole world thou canst find,
That heart I'll give to thee.

Bid that heart stay, and it will stay,
To honor thy decrees;
Or bid it languish quite away,
And 't shall do so for thee.

Bid me to weep, and I will weep,
While I have eyes to see;
And, having none, yet I will keep
A heart to weep for thee.

Bid me despair and I'll despair,
Under that cypress tree;
Or bid me die, and I will dare
E'en death, to die for thee.

Thou art my life, my love, my heart,
The very eyes of me;
And hast command of every part,
To live and die for thee.

Robert Herrick (1591-1674)

Upon Julia's Clothes

Whenas in silks my Julia goes,
Then, then, methinks, how sweetly flows
The liquefaction of her clothes.

Next, when I cast mine eyes and see
That brave vibration each way free,
Oh, how that glittering taketh me!

Robert Herrick (1591-1674)

A Divine Rapture

E'en like two little bank-dividing brooks,
That wash the pebbles with their wanton streams,
And having ranged and search'd a thousand nooks,
Meet both at length in silver-breasted Thames,
Where in a greater current they conjoin:
So I my Best-beloved's am; so He is mine.

E'en so we met; and after long pursuit,
E'en so we joined; we both became entire;
No need for either to renew a suit,
For I was flax, and He was flames of fire:
Our firm-united souls did more than twine;
So I my Best-beloved's am; so He is mine.

If all those glittering Monarchs, that command
The servile quarters of this earthly ball,
Should tender in exchange their shares of land,
I would not change my fortunes for them all:
Their wealth is but a counter to my coin:
The world 's but theirs; but my Beloved's mine.

Francis Quarles (1592-1644)

Love (III)

Love bade me welcome: yet my soul drew back,
Guilty of dust and sin.
But quick-eyed Love, observing me grow slack
From my first entrance in,
Drew nearer to me, sweetly questioning
If I lacked anything.

"A guest," I answered, "worthy to be here":
Love said, "You shall be he."
"I, the unkind, ungrateful? Ah, my dear,
I cannot look on thee."
Love took my hand, and smiling did reply,
"Who made the eyes but I?"

"Truth, Lord; but I have marred them; let my shame
Go where it doth deserve."
"And know you not," says Love, "who bore the blame?"
"My dear, then I will serve."
"You must sit down," says Love, "and taste my meat."
So I did sit and eat.

George Herbert (1593-1633)

To My Dear and Loving Husband

If ever two were one, then surely we.
If ever man were lov'd by wife, then thee;
If ever wife was happy in a man,
Compare with me ye women if you can.
I prize thy love more then whole mines of gold,
Or all the riches that the East doth hold.
My love is such that rivers cannot quench,
Nor ought but love from thee, give recompence.
Thy love is such I can no way repay,
The heavens reward thee manifold I pray.
Then while we live, in love let's so persevere,
That when we live no more, we may live ever.

Anne Bradstreet (1612-1672)

To Althea, from Prison

When love with unconfined wings
. . . Hovers within my gates,
And my divine Althea brings
. . . To whisper at the grates;
When I lie tangled in her hair
. . . And fettered to her eye,
The birds that wanton in the air
. . . Know no such liberty.
When flowing cups run swiftly round
. . . With no allaying Thames,
Our careless heads with roses bound,
. . . Our hearts with loyal flames;
When thirst grief in wine we steep,
. . . When healths and draughts go free,
Fishes that tipple in the deep
. . . Know no such liberty . . .
Stone walls do not a prison make,
. . . Nor iron bars a cage;
Minds innocent and quiet take
. . . That for an hermitage;
If I have freedom in my love,
. . . And in my soul am free,
Angels alone, that soar above,
Enjoy such liberty.

Richard Lovelace (1618-1657)

To Amarantha, That She Would Dishevel Her Hair

Amarantha sweet and fair
Ah braid no more that shining hair!
As my curious hand or eye
Hovering round thee let it fly.

Let it fly as unconfin'd
As its calm ravisher, the wind,
Who hath left his darling th'East,
To wanton o'er that spicy nest.

Ev'ry tress must be confest
But neatly tangled at the best;
Like a clue of golden thread,
Most excellently ravelled.

Do not then wind up that light
In ribands, and o'er-cloud in night;
Like the sun in's early ray,
But shake your head and scatter day.

See 'tis broke! Within this grove
The bower, and the walks of love,
Weary lie we down and rest,
And fan each other's panting breast.

Here we'll strip and cool our fire
In cream below, in milk-baths higher:
And when all wells are drawn dry,
I'll drink a tear out of thine eye,

Which our very joys shall leave
That sorrows thus we can deceive;
Or our very sorrows weep,
That joys so ripe, so little keep.

Richard Lovelace (1618-1657)

To His Coy Mistress

Had we but world enough, and time,
This coyness, lady, were no crime.
We would sit down and think which way
To walk, and pass our long love's day;
Thou by the Indian Ganges' side
Shouldst rubies find; I by the tide
Of Humber would complain. I would
Love you ten years before the Flood;
And you should, if you please, refuse
Till the conversion of the Jews.
My vegetable love should grow
Vaster than empires, and more slow.
An hundred years should go to praise
Thine eyes, and on thy forehead gaze;
Two hundred to adore each breast,
But thirty thousand to the rest;
An age at least to every part,
And the last age should show your heart.
For, lady, you deserve this state,
Nor would I love at lower rate.

But at my back I always hear
Time's winged chariot hurrying near;
And yonder all before us lie
Deserts of vast eternity.
Thy beauty shall no more be found,
Nor, in thy marble vault, shall sound
My echoing song; then worms shall try
That long preserv'd virginity,
And your quaint honour turn to dust,
And into ashes all my lust.
The grave's a fine and private place,
But none I think do there embrace.

Now therefore, while the youthful hue
Sits on thy skin like morning dew,
And while thy willing soul transpires
At every pore with instant fires,
Now let us sport us while we may;

And now, like am'rous birds of prey,
Rather at once our time devour,
Than languish in his slow-chapp'd power.
Let us roll all our strength, and all
Our sweetness, up into one ball;
And tear our pleasures with rough strife
Thorough the iron gates of life.
Thus, though we cannot make our sun
Stand still, yet we will make him run.

Andrew Marvell (1621-1678)

The Definition of Love

My love is of a birth as rare
As 'tis for object strange and high;
It was begotten by Despair
Upon Impossibility.

Magnanimous Despair alone
Could show me so divine a thing
Where feeble Hope could ne'er have flown,
But vainly flapp'd its tinsel wing.

And yet I quickly might arrive
Where my extended soul is fixt,
But Fate does iron wedges drive,
And always crowds itself betwixt.

For Fate with jealous eye does see
Two perfect loves, nor lets them close;
Their union would her ruin be,
And her tyrannic pow'r depose.

And therefore her decrees of steel
Us as the distant poles have plac'd,
(Though love's whole world on us doth wheel)
Not by themselves to be embrac'd;

Unless the giddy heaven fall,
And earth some new convulsion tear;
And, us to join, the world should all
Be cramp'd into a planisphere.

As lines, so loves oblique may well
Themselves in every angle greet;
But ours so truly parallel,
Though infinite, can never meet.

Therefore the love which us doth bind,
But Fate so enviously debars,
Is the conjunction of the mind,
And opposition of the stars.

Andrew Marvell (1621-1678)

On Her Loving Two Equally

I

How strong does my passion flow,
Divided equally twixt two?
Damon had ne'er subdued my heart
Had not Alexis took his part;
Nor could Alexis powerful prove,
Without my Damon's aid, to gain my love.

II

When my Alexis present is,
Then I for Damon sigh and mourn;
But when Alexis I do miss,
Damon gains nothing but my scorn.
But if it chance they both are by,
For both alike I languish, sigh, and die.

III

Cure then, thou might wing'd god,
This restless fever in my blood;
One golden-pointed dart take back:
But which, O Cupid, wilt thou take?
If Damon's, all my hopes are crossed;
Or that of my Alexis, I am lost.

Aphra Behn (1640-1689)

To a Young Lady

Sweet stream that winds through yonder glade,
Apt emblem of a virtuous maid!
Silent and chaste she steals along,
Far from the world's gay busy throng:
With gentle yet prevailing force,
Intent upon her destined course;
Graceful and useful all she does,
Blessing and blest where'er she goes;
Pure-bosom'd as that watery glass,
And Heaven reflected in her face.

William Cowper (1731-1800)

Lucy

Strange fits of passion have I known:
And I will dare to tell,
But in the lover's ear alone,
What once to me befell.

When she I loved look'd every day
Fresh as a rose in June,
I to her cottage bent my way,
Beneath an evening moon.

Upon the moon I fix'd my eye,
All over the wide lea;
With quickening pace my horse drew nigh
Those paths so dear to me.

And now we reach'd the orchard-plot;
And, as we climb'd the hill,
The sinking moon to Lucy's cot
Came near and nearer still.

In one of those sweet dreams I slept,
Kind Nature's gentlest boon!
And all the while my eyes I kept
On the descending moon.

My horse moved on; hoof after hoof
He raised, and never stopp'd:
When down behind the cottage roof,
At once, the bright moon dropp'd.

What fond and wayward thoughts will slide
Into a lover's head!
'O mercy!' to myself I cried,
'If Lucy should be dead!'

William Wordsworth (1770-1850)

The Presence of Love

And in Life's noisiest hour,
There whispers still the ceaseless Love of Thee,
The heart's Self-solace and soliloquy.

You mould my Hopes, you fashion me within;
And to the leading Love-throb in the Heart
Thro' all my Being, thro' my pulse's beat;
You lie in all my many Thoughts, like Light,
Like the fair light of Dawn, or summer Eve
On rippling Stream, or cloud-reflecting Lake.

And looking to the Heaven, that bends above you,
How oft! I bless the Lot that made me love you.

Samuel Taylor Coleridge (1772-1834)

Rose Aylmer

Ah, what avails the sceptred race!
Ah, what the form divine!
What every virtue, every grace!
Rose Aylmer, all were thine.

Rose Aylmer, whom these wakeful eyes
May weep, but never see,
A night of memories and sighs
I consecrate to thee.

Walter Savage Landor (1775-1864)

Proud Word You Never Spoke

Proud word you never spoke, but you will speak
Four not exempt from pride some future day.
Resting on one white hand a warm wet cheek,
Over my open volume you will say,
'This man loved me'—then rise and trip away.

Walter Savage Landor (1775-1864)

Did Not

'Twas a new feeling - something more
Than we had dared to own before,
Which then we hid not;
We saw it in each other's eye,
And wished, in every half-breathed sigh,
To speak, but did not.

She felt my lips' impassioned touch -
'Twas the first time I dared so much,
And yet she chid not;
But whispered o'er my burning brow,
'Oh, do you doubt I love you now?'
Sweet soul! I did not.

Warmly I felt her bosom thrill,
I pressed it closer, closer still,
Though gently bid not;
Till - oh! the world hath seldom heard
Of lovers, who so nearly erred,
And yet, who did not.

Thomas Moore (1779-1852)

Believe Me, If All These Endearing Young Charms

Believe me, if all those endearing young charms
Which I gaze on so fondly today
Were to change by tomorrow and fleet in my arms
Like fairy gifts fading away,
Thou wouldst still be adored as this moment thou art
Let thy loveliness fade as it will
And around the dear ruin each wish of my heart
Would entwine itself verdantly still.

It is not while beauty and youth are thine own
And thy cheeks unprofaned by a tear
That the fervor and faith of a soul can be known
To which time will but make thee more dear.
No, the heart that has truly loved never forgets
But as truly loves on to the close
As the sunflower turns to her God when he sets
The same look which she turned when he rose.

Thomas Moore (1779-1852)

Jenny Kissed Me

Jenny kissed me when we met,
Jumping from the chair she sat in.
Time, you thief, who love to get
Sweets into your list, put that in.
Say I'm weary, say I'm sad;
Say that health and wealth have missed me;
Say I'm growing old, but add—
Jenny kissed me!

James Henry Leigh Hunt (1784-1859)

She Walks in Beauty

1

She walks in beauty, like the night
Of cloudless climes and starry skies;
And all that's best of dark and bright
Meet in her aspect and her eyes:
Thus mellow'd to that tender light
Which heaven to gaudy day denies.

2

One shade the more, one ray the less,
Had half impair'd the nameless grace
Which waves in every raven tress,
Or softly lightens o'er her face;
Where thoughts serenely sweet express
How pure, how dear their dwelling place.

3

And on that cheek, and o'er that brow,
So soft, so calm, yet eloquent,
The smiles that win, the tints that glow,
But tell of days in goodness spent,
A mind at peace with all below,
A heart whose love is innocent!

Lord George Gordon Byron (1788-1824)

The Indian Serenade

I arise from dreams of thee
In the first sweet sleep of night,
When the winds are breathing low,
And the stars are shining bright.
I arise from dreams of thee,
And a spirit in my feet
Hath led me—who knows how?
To thy chamber window, Sweet!

The wandering airs they faint
On the dark, the silent stream—
And the champak's odours
Like sweet thoughts in a dream;
The nightingale's complaint,
It dies upon her heart,
As I must on thine,
O beloved as thou art!

O lift me from the grass!
I die! I faint! I fail!
Let thy love in kisses rain
On my lips and eyelids pale.
My cheek is cold and white, alas!
My heart beats loud and fast:
O press it to thine own again,
Where it will break at last!

Percy Bysshe Shelley (1792-1822)

First Love

I ne'er was struck before that hour
With love so sudden and so sweet.
Her face it bloomed like a sweet flower
And stole my heart away complete.

My face turned pale, a deadly pale.
My legs refused to walk away,
And when she looked what could I ail
My life and all seemed turned to clay.

And then my blood rushed to my face
And took my eyesight quite away.
The trees and bushes round the place
Seemed midnight at noonday.

I could not see a single thing,
Words from my eyes did start.
They spoke as chords do from the string,
And blood burnt round my heart.

Are flowers the winter's choice
Is love's bed always snow
She seemed to hear my silent voice
Not love appeals to know.

I never saw so sweet a face
As that I stood before.
My heart has left its dwelling place
And can return no more.

John Clare (1793-1864)

Song [Secret Love]

I hid my love when young while I
Couldn't bear the buzzing of a fly
I hid my love to my despite
Till I could not bear to look at light
I dare not gaze upon her face
But left her memory in each place
Where ere I saw a wild flower lie
I kissed and bade my love goodbye

I met her in the greenest dells
Where dew drops pearl the wood bluebells
The lost breeze kissed her bright blue eye
The bee kissed and went singing by
A sunbeam found a passage there
A gold chain round her neck so fair
As secret as the wild bee's song
She lay there all the summer long

I hid my love in field and town
Till e'en the breeze would knock me down
The bees seemed singing ballads l'er
The fly's buss turned a Lion's roar
And even silence found a tongue
To haunt me all the summer long
The riddle nature could not prove
Was nothing else but secret love

John Clare (1793-1864)

O love me truly!

You say you love; but with a voice
Chaster than a nun's, who singeth
    The soft vespers to herself
    While the chime-bell ringeth—
        O love me truly!

You say you love; but with a smile
    Cold as sunrise in September,
    As you were Saint Cupid's nun,
    And kept his weeks of Ember—
        O love me truly!

You say you love; but then your lips
    Coral tinted teach no blisses,
    More than coral in the sea—
    They never pout for kisses—
        O love me truly!

You say you love; but then your hand
No soft squeeze for squeeze returneth;
    It is, like a statue's, dead,—
    While mine to passion burneth—
        O love me truly!

    O breathe a word or two of fire!
Smile, as if those words should burn me,
    Squeeze as lovers should—O kiss
    And in thy heart inurn me—
        O love me truly!

John Keats (1795-1821)

Bright Star, Would I Were Steadfast as Thou Art

Bright star, would I were steadfast as thou art—
Not in lone splendour hung aloft the night,
And watching, with eternal lids apart,
Like nature's patient sleepless eremite,
The moving waters at their priestlike task
Of pure ablution round earth's human shores,
Or gazing on the new soft-fallen mask
Of snow upon the mountains and the moors;
No—yet still steadfast, still unchangeable,
Pillow'd upon my fair love's ripening breast,
To feel for ever its soft fall and swell,
Awake for ever in a sweet unrest,
Still, still to hear her tender-taken breath,
And so live ever—or else swoon to death.

John Keats (1795-1821)

She Is Not Fair To Outward View

She is not fair to outward view
As many maidens be,
Her loveliness I never knew
Until she smiled on me;
O, then I saw her eye was bright,
A well of love, a spring of light!

But now her looks are coy and cold,
To mine they ne'er reply,
And yet I cease not to behold
The love-light in her eye:
Her very frowns are fairer far
Than smiles of other maidens are.

Hartley Coleridge (1796-1849)

Ruth

She stood breast high amid the corn,
Clasped by the golden light of morn,
Like the sweetheart of the sun,
Who many a glowing kiss had won.
On her cheek an autumn flush,
Deeply ripened; such a blush
In the midst of brown was born,
Like red poppies grown with corn.
Round her eyes her tresses fell,
Which were blackest none could tell,
But long lashes veiled a light,
That had else been all too bright.
And her hat, with shady brim,
Made her tressy forehead dim;
Thus she stood amid the stooks,
Praising God with sweetest looks:
Sure, I said, heaven did not mean,
Where I reap thou shouldst but glean,
Lay thy sheaf adown and come,
Share my harvest and my home.

Thomas Hood (1799-1845)

I Love Thee

I love thee, as I love the calm
Of sweet, star-lighted hours!
I love thee, as I love the balm
Of early jes'mine flow'rs.

I love thee, as I love the last
Rich smile of fading day,
Which lingereth, like the look we cast,
On rapture pass'd away.

I love thee as I love the tone
Of some soft-breathing flute
Whose soul is wak'd for me alone,
When all beside is mute.

I love thee as I love the first
Young violet of the spring;
Or the pale lily, April-nurs'd,
To scented blossoming.

I love thee, as I love the full,
Clear gushings of the song,
Which lonely--sad--and beautiful--
At night-fall floats along,

Pour'd by the bul-bul forth to greet
The hours of rest and dew;
When melody and moonlight meet
To blend their charm, and hue.

I love thee, as the glad bird loves
The freedom of its wing,
On which delightedly it moves
In wildest wandering.

I love thee as I love the swell,
And hush, of some low strain,
Which bringeth, by its gentle spell,
The past to life again.

Such is the feeling which from thee
Nought earthly can allure:
'Tis ever link'd to all I see
Of gifted--high--and pure!

Eliza Acton (1799-1859)

How Do I Love Thee

How do I love thee? Let me count the ways.
I love thee to the depth and breadth and height
My soul can reach, when feeling out of sight
For the ends of Being and ideal Grace.
I love thee to the level of everyday's
Most quiet need, by sun and candle-light.
I love thee freely, as men strive for Right;
I love thee purely, as they turn from Praise.
I love thee with a passion put to use
In my old griefs, and with my childhood's faith.
I love thee with a love I seemed to lose
With my lost saints, --- I love thee with the breath,
Smiles, tears, of all my life! --- and, if God choose,
I shall but love thee better after death.

Elizabeth Barrett Browning (1806-1861)

Sonnets from the Portuguese, 14

If thou must love me, let it be for nought
Except for love's sake only. Do not say
'I love her for her smile---her look---her way
Of speaking gently,---for a trick of thought
That falls in well with mine, and certes brought
A sense of pleasant ease on such a day'---
For these things in themselves, Belovèd, may
Be changed, or change for thee,---and love, so wrought,
May be unwrought so. Neither love me for
Thine own dear pity's wiping my cheeks dry,---
A creature might forget to weep, who bore
Thy comfort long, and lose thy love thereby!
But love me for love's sake, that evermore
Thou mayst love on, through love's eternity.

Elizabeth Barrett Browning (1806-1861)

How do I love thee? Let me count the ways.

How do I love thee? Let me count the ways.
I love thee to the depth and breadth and height
My soul can reach, when feeling out of sight
For the ends of Being and ideal Grace.
I love thee to the level of everyday's
Most quiet need, by sun and candle-light.
I love thee freely, as men strive for Right;
I love thee purely, as they turn from Praise.
I love thee with a passion put to use
In my old griefs, and with my childhood's faith.
I love thee with a love I seemed to lose
With my lost saints, --- I love thee with the breath,
Smiles, tears, of all my life! --- and, if God choose,
I shall but love thee better after death.

Elizabeth Barrett Browning (1806-1861)

Now Sleeps the Crimson Petal

Now sleeps the crimson petal, now the white;
Nor waves the cypress in the palace walk;
Nor winks the gold fin in the porphyry font:
The firefly wakens: waken thou with me.
Now droops the milkwhite peacock like a ghost,
And like a ghost she glimmers on to me.
Now lies the Earth all Danae to the stars,
And all thy heart lies open unto me.
Now slides the silent meteor on, and leaves
A shining furrow, as thy thoughts in me.
Now folds the lily all her sweetness up,
And slips into the bosom of the lake:
So fold thyself, my dearest, thou, and slip
Into my bosom and be lost in me.

Lord Alfred Tennyson (1809-1892)

Marriage Morning

Light, so low upon earth,
You send a flash to the sun.
Here is the golden close of love,
All my wooing is done.
Oh, the woods and the meadows,
Woods where we hid from the wet,
Stiles where we stay'd to be kind,
Meadows in which we met!

Light, so low in the vale
You flash and lighten afar,
For this is the golden morning of love,
And you are his morning star.
Flash, I am coming, I come,
By meadow and stile and wood,
Oh, lighten into my eyes and heart,
Into my heart and my blood!

Heart, are you great enough
For a love that never tires?
O' heart, are you great enough for love?
I have heard of thorns and briers,
Over the meadow and stiles,
Over the world to the end of it
Flash for a million miles.

Lord Alfred Tennyson (1809-1892)

Serenade

So sweet the hour, so calm the time,
I feel it more than half a crime,
When Nature sleeps and stars are mute,
To mar the silence ev'n with lute.
At rest on ocean's brilliant dyes
An image of Elysium lies:
Seven Pleiades entranced in Heaven,
Form in the deep another seven:
Endymion nodding from above
Sees in the sea a second love.
Within the valleys dim and brown,
And on the spectral mountain's crown,
The wearied light is dying down,
And earth, and stars, and sea, and sky
Are redolent of sleep, as I
Am redolent of thee and thine
Enthralling love, my Adeline.
But list, O list, - so soft and low
Thy lover's voice tonight shall flow,
That, scarce awake, thy soul shall deem
My words the music of a dream.
Thus, while no single sound too rude
Upon thy slumber shall intrude,
Our thoughts, our souls - O God above!
In every deed shall mingle, love.

Edgar Allan Poe (1809-1849)

To Helen

I saw thee once - once only - years ago:
I must not say how many - but not many.
It was a July midnight; and from out
A full-orbed moon, that, like thine own soul, soaring,
Sought a precipitate pathway up through heaven,
There fell a silvery-silken veil of light,
With quietude, and sultriness, and slumber,
Upon the upturned faces of a thousand
Roses that grew in an enchanted garden,
Where no wind dared to stir, unless on tiptoe
Fell on the upturn'd faces of these roses
That gave out, in return for the love-light,
Their odorous souls in an ecstatic death
Fell on the upturn'd faces of these roses
That smiled and died in this parterre, enchanted
By thee, and by the poetry of thy presence.

Edgar Allan Poe (1809-1849)

Eulalie

I dwelt alone
In a world of moan,
And my soul was a stagnant tide,
Till the fair and gentle Eulalie became my blushing bride—
Till the yellow-haired young Eulalie became my smiling bride.

Ah, less—less bright
The stars of the night
Than the eyes of the radiant girl!
That the vapor can make
With the moon-tints of purple and pearl,
Can vie with the modest Eulalie's most unregarded curl—
Can compare with the bright-eyed Eulalie's most humble and careless curl.

Now Doubt—now Pain
Come never again,
For her soul gives me sigh for sigh,
And all day long
Shines, bright and strong,
Astarte within the sky,
While ever to her dear Eulalie upturns her matron eye—
While ever to her young Eulalie upturns her violet eye.

Edgar Allan Poe (1809-1849)

A Pretty Woman

That fawn-skin-dappled hair of hers,
And the blue eye
Dear and dewy,
And that infantine fresh air of hers!

To think men cannot take you, Sweet,
And enfold you,
Ay, and hold you,
And so keep you what they make you, Sweet!

You like us for a glance, you know---
For a word's sake
Or a sword's sake,
All's the same, whate'er the chance, you know.

And in turn we make you ours, we say---
You and youth too,
Eyes and mouth too,
All the face composed of flowers, we say.

All's our own, to make the most of, Sweet---
Sing and say for,
Watch and pray for,
Keep a secret or go boast of, Sweet!

But for loving, why, you would not, Sweet,
Though we prayed you,
Paid you, brayed you
in a mortar---for you could not, Sweet!

So, we leave the sweet face fondly there:
Be its beauty
Its sole duty!
Let all hope of grace beyond, lie there!

And while the face lies quiet there,
Who shall wonder
That I ponder
A conclusion? I will try it there.

As---why must one, for the love foregone,
Scout mere liking?
Thunder-striking
Earth---the heaven, we looked above for, gone!

Why, with beauty, needs there money be,
Love with liking?
Crush the fly-king
In his gauze, because no honey-bee?

May not liking be so simple-sweet,
If love grew there
'Twould undo there
All that breaks the cheek to dimples sweet?

Is the creature too imperfect,
Would you mend it
And so end it?
Since not all addition perfects aye!

Or is it of its kind, perhaps,
Just perfection---
Whence, rejection
Of a grace not to its mind, perhaps?

Shall we burn up, tread that face at once
Into tinder,
And so hinder
Sparks from kindling all the place at once?

Or else kiss away one's soul on her?
Your love-fancies!
---A sick man sees
Truer, when his hot eyes roll on her!

Thus the craftsman thinks to grace the rose---
Plucks a mould-flower
For his gold flower,
Uses fine things that efface the rose:

Rosy rubies make its cup more rose,
Precious metals
Ape the petals,---
Last, some old king locks it up, morose!

Then how grace a rose? I know a way!
Leave it, rather.
Must you gather?
Smell, kiss, wear it---at last, throw away!

Robert Browning (1812-1889)

Life in a Love

Escape me?
Never—
Beloved!
While I am I, and you are you,
So long as the world contains us both,
Me the loving and you the loth,
While the one eludes, must the other pursue.
My life is a fault at last, I fear:
It seems too much like a fate, indeed!
Though I do my best I shall scarce succeed.
But what if I fail of my purpose here?
It is but to keep the nerves at strain,
To dry one's eyes and laugh at a fall,
And baffled, get up to begin again,—
So the chase takes up one's life, that's all.
While, look but once from your farthest bound,
At me so deep in the dust and dark,
No sooner the old hope drops to ground
Than a new one, straight to the selfsame mark,
I shape me—
Ever
Removed!

Robert Browning (1812-1889)

Meeting at Night

1

The gray sea and the long black land;
And the yellow half-moon large and low;
And the startled little waves that leap
In fiery ringlets from their sleep,
As I gain the cove with pushing prow,
And quench its speed i' the slushy sand.
2
Then a mile of warm sea-scented beach;
Three fields to cross till a farm appears;
A tap at the pane, the quick sharp scratch
And blue spurt of a lighted match,
And a voice less loud, through its joys and fears,
Than the two hearts beating each to each!

Robert Browning (1812-1889)

Love in a Life

Room after room,
I hunt the house through
We inhabit together.
Heart, fear nothing, for, heart, thou shalt find her--
Next time, herself!--not the trouble behind her
Left in the curtain, the couch's perfume!
As she brushed it, the cornice-wreath blossomed anew:
Yon looking-glass gleaned at the wave of her feather.

Yet the day wears,
And door succeeds door;
I try the fresh fortune--
Range the wide house from the wing to the centre.
Still the same chance! She goes out as I enter.
Spend my whole day in the quest--who cares?
But 'tis twilight, you see--with such suites to explore,
Such closets to search, such alcoves to importune!

Robert Browning (1812-1889)

Beautiful Dreamer

Beautiful dreamer, wake unto me,
Starlight and dewdrops are waiting for thee;
Sounds of the rude world heard in the day,
Lull'd by the moonlight have all pass'd away!

Beautiful dreamer, queen of my song,
List while I woo thee with soft melody;
Gone are the cares of life's busy throng.

Beautiful dreamer, awake unto me!
Beautiful dreamer, awake unto me!

Beautiful dreamer, out on the sea,
Mermaids are chaunting the wild lorelie;
Over the streamlet vapors are borne,
Waiting to fade at the bright coming morn.

Beautiful dreamer, beam on my heart,
E'en as the morn on the streamlet and sea;
Then will all clouds of sorrow depart,

Beautiful dreamer, awake unto me!

Stephen Foster (1826-1864)

Sonnet 23: Love's Baubles

I stood where Love in brimming armfuls bore
Slight wanton flowers and foolish toys of fruit:
And round him ladies thronged in warm pursuit,
Fingered and lipped and proffered the strange store.
And from one hand the petal and the core
Savoured of sleep; and cluster and curled shoot
Seemed from another hand like shame's salute,
Gifts that I felt my cheek was blushing for.

At last Love bade my Lady give the same:
And as I looked, the dew was light thereon;
And as I took them, at her touch they shone
With inmost heaven-hue of the heart of flame.
And then Love said: "Lo! when the hand is hers,
Follies of love are love's true ministers."

Dante Gabriel Rossetti (1828-1882)

The Blessed Damozel

The blessed damozel leaned out
From the gold bar of Heaven;
Her eyes were deeper than the depth
Of waters stilled at even;
She had three lilies in her hand,
And the stars in her hair were seven.
Her robe, ungirt from clasp to hem,
No wrought flowers did adorn,
But a white rose of Mary's gift,
For service meetly worn;
Her hair that lay along her back
Was yellow like ripe corn.
Herseemed she scarce had been a day
One of God's choristers;

The wonder was not yet quite gone
From that still look of hers;
Albeit, to them she left, her day
Had counted as ten years.
(To one, it is ten years of years.
. . . Yet now, and in this place,
Surely she leaned o'er me — her hair
Fell all about my face. . . .
Nothing: the autumn-fall of leaves.
The whole year sets apace.)
It was the rampart of God's house
That she was standing on;
By God built over the sheer depth
The which is Space begun;
So high, that looking downward thence
She scarce could see the sun.
It lies in Heaven, across the flood
Of ether, as a bridge.
Beneath, the tides of day and night
With flame and darkness ridge
The void, as low as where this earth
Spins like a fretful midge.

Around her, lovers, newly met

'Mid deathless love's acclaims,
   Spoke evermore among themselves
     Their heart-remembered names;
   And the souls mounting up to God
     Went by her like thin flames.
And still she bowed herself and stooped
     Out of the circling charm;
   Until her bosom must have made
     The bar she leaned on warm,
   And the lilies lay as if asleep
     Along her bended arm.
From the fixed place of Heaven she saw
     Time like a pulse shake fierce
Through all the worlds. Her gaze still strove
     Within the gulf to pierce
Its path; and now she spoke as when
     The stars sang in their spheres.
The sun was gone now; the curled moon
     Was like a little feather
Fluttering far down the gulf; and now
   She spoke through the still weather.

Her voice was like the voice of the stars
     Had when they sang together.
(Ah sweet! Even now, in that bird's song,
     Strove not her accents there,
Fain to be hearkened? When those bells
     Possessed the mid-day air,
Strove not her steps to reach my side
     Down all the echoing stair?)
'I wish that he were come to me,
     For he will come,' she said.
Lord, Lord, has he not pray'd?
Are not two prayers a perfect strength?
     And shall I feel afraid?
'When round his head the aureole clings,
     And he is clothed in white,
I'll take his hand and go with him
     To the deep wells of light;
As unto a stream we will step down,
     And bathe there in God's sight.
'We two will stand beside that shrine,
     Occult, withheld, untrod,

Whose lamps are stirred continually
    With prayer sent up to God;
                And see our old prayers, granted, melt
                    Each like a little cloud.
            'We two will lie i' the shadow of
                    That living mystic tree
        Within whose secret growth the Dove
                    Is sometimes felt to be,
        While every leaf that His plumes touch
                Saith His Name audibly.
            'And I myself will teach to him,
                    I myself, lying so,
        The songs I sing here; which his voice
                Shall pause in, hushed and slow,
        And find some knowledge at each pause,
                Or some new thing to know.'
            (Alas! We two, we two, thou say'st!
                Yea, one wast thou with me
            That once of old. But shall God lift
                    To endless unity
                Was but its love for thee?)

            'We two,' she said, 'will seek the groves
                Where the lady Mary is,
        With her five handmaidens, whose names
                Are five sweet symphonies,
            Cecily, Gertrude, Magdalen,
                Margaret and Rosalys.
        'Circlewise sit they, with bound locks
                And foreheads garlanded;
        Into the fine cloth white like flame
                Weaving the golden thread,
        To fashion the birth-robes for them
                Who are just born, being dead.
        'He shall fear, haply, and be dumb:
                Then will I lay my cheek
        To his, and tell about our love,
                Not once abashed or weak:
        And the dear Mother will approve
                My pride, and let me speak.
        'Herself shall bring us, hand in hand,
                To him round whom all souls
    Kneel, the clear-ranged unnumbered heads
                Bowed with their aureoles:

And angels meeting us shall sing
  To their citherns and citoles.
'There will I ask of Christ the Lord
  Thus much for him and me: —
Only to live as once on earth
  With Love, — only to be,
As then awhile, for ever now
  Together, I and he.'
She gazed and listened and then said,
  Less sad of speech than mild, —
'All this is when he comes.' She ceased.
  The light thrilled towards her, fill'd
With angels in strong level flight.
  Her eyes prayed, and she smil'd.
(I saw her smile.) But soon their path
  Was vague in distant spheres:
And then she cast her arms along
  The golden barriers,
And laid her face between her hands,
  And wept. (I heard her tears.)

Dante Gabriel Rossetti (1828-1882)

Without Her

What of her glass without her? The blank grey
There where the pool is blind of the moon's face.
Her dress without her? The tossed empty space
Of cloud-rack whence the moon has passed away.
Her paths without her? Day's appointed sway
Usurped by desolate night. Her pillowed place
Without her? Tears, ah me! for love's good grace,
And cold forgetfulness of night or day.

What of the heart without her? Nay, poor heart,
Of thee what word remains ere speech be still?
A wayfarer by barren ways and chill,
Steep ways and weary, without her thou art,
Where the long cloud, the long wood's counterpart,
Sheds doubled darkness up the labouring hill.

Dante Gabriel Rossetti (1828-1882)

Silent Noon

Your hands lie open in the long fresh grass,--
...The finger-points look through like rosy blooms:
...Your eyes smile peace. The pasture gleams and glooms
'Neath billowing skies that scatter and amass.
All round our nest, far as the eye can pass,
...Are golden kingcup-fields with silver edge
...Where the cow-parsley skirts the hawthorn-hedge.
'Tis visible silence, still as the hour-glass.
Deep in the sun-searched growths the dragon-fly
Hangs like a blue thread loosened from the sky:--
...So this wing'd hour is dropt to us from above.
Oh! clasp we to our hearts, for deathless dower,
This close-companioned inarticulate hour
...When twofold silence was the song of love.

Dante Gabriel Rossetti (1828-1882)

I gave myself to him

I gave myself to him,
And took himself for pay.
The solemn contract of a life
Was ratified this way

The value might disappoint,
Myself a poorer prove
Than this my purchaser suspect,
The daily own of Love

Depreciates the sight;
But, 'til the merchant buy,
Still fabled, in the isles of spice
The subtle cargoes lie.

At least, 'tis mutual risk,
Some found it mutual gain;
Sweet debt of Life, each night to owe,
Insolvent, every noon.

Emily Dickinson (1830-1886)

At Last

At last, when all the summer shine
That warmed life's early hours is past,
Your loving fingers seek for mine
And hold them close at last at last!
Not oft the robin comes to build
Its nest upon the leafless bough
By autumn robbed, by winter chilled,
But you, dear heart, you love me now.

Though there are shadows on my brow
And furrows on my cheek, in truth,
The marks where Time's remorseless plough
Broke up the blooming sward of Youth,
Though fled is every girlish grace
Might win or hold a lover's vow,
Despite my sad and faded face,
And darkened heart, you love me now!

I count no more my wasted tears;
They left no echo of their fall;
I mourn no more my lonesome years;
This blessed hour atones for all.
I fear not all that Time or Fate
May bring to burden heart or brow,
Strong in the love that came so late,
Our souls shall keep it always now!

Elizabeth Akers Allen (1832-1867)

Annie Laurie

Maxwelton's hills are bonnie
Where early falls the dew
And 'twas there that Annie Laurie
Gived me her promise true.
Gived me her promise true
Which ne'er forgot shall be
And for bonnie Annie Laurie
I'd lay me down and die.

Her brow is like the snow drift,
Her throat is like the swan,
Her face, it is the fairest
That e'er the sun shone on.
That e'er the sun shone on
And dark blue are her eyes
And for bonnie Annie Laurie
I'd lay me down and die.

Like dew on the daisy lyin'
Is the fall of her fairy feet
And like winds in summer sighing
Her voice is low and sweet.
Her voice is low and sweet
And she's all the world to me
And for bonnie Annie Laurie
I'd lay me down and die.

William Douglas (1832-1889)

Love's Trinity

Soul, heart, and body, we thus singly name,
Are not in love divisible and distinct,
But each with each inseparably link'd.
One is not honour, and the other shame,
But burn as closely fused as fuel, heat, and flame.

They do not love who give the body and keep
The heart ungiven; nor they who yield the soul,
And guard the body. Love doth give the whole;
Its range being high as heaven, as ocean deep,
Wide as the realms of air or planet's curving sweep.

Alfred Austin (1835-1913)

Evening Song

Look off, dear Love, across the sallow sands,
And mark yon meeting of the sun and sea;
How long they kiss in sight of all the lands,
Ah! longer, longer we.

Now, in the sea's red vintage melts the sun
As Egypt's pearl dissolved in rosy wine
And Cleopatra night drinks all. 'Tis done,
Love, lay thine hand in mine.

Come forth, sweet stars, and comfort heaven's heart,
Glimmer, ye waves, 'round else unlighted sands;
Oh night! divorce our sun and sky apart
Never our lips, our hands.

Sidney Lanier (1842-1881)

An Evening Song

Look off, dear Love, across the sallow sands,
And mark yon meeting of the sun and sea,
How long they kiss in sight of all the lands.
Ah! longer, longer, we.
Now in the sea's red vintage melts the sun,
As Egypt's pearl dissolved in rosy wine,
And Cleopatra night drinks all. 'Tis done,
Love, lay thine hand in mine.
Come forth, sweet stars, and comfort heaven's heart;
Glimmer, ye waves, round else unlighted sands.
O night! divorce our sun and sky apart
Never our lips, our hands.

Sidney Lanier (1842-1881)

The Lost Thrill

I grow so weary, someway, of all things
That love and loving have vouchsafed to me,
Since now all dreamed-of sweets of ecstasy
Am I possessed of: The caress that clings—
The lips that mix with mine with murmurings
No language may interpret, and the free,
Unfettered brood of kisses, hungrily
Feasting in swarms on honeyed blossomings
Of passion's fullest flower—For yet I miss
The essence that alone makes love divine—
The subtle flavoring no tang of this
Weak wine of melody may here define:—
A something found and lost in the first kiss
A lover ever poured through lips of mine.

James Whitcomb Riley (1847-1916)

A Valentine to My Wife

Accept, dear girl, this little token,
And if between the lines you seek,
You'll find the love I've often spoken-
The love my dying lips shall speak.

Our little ones are making merry
O'er am'rous ditties rhymed in jest,
But in these words (though awkward-very)
The genuine article's expressed.

You are as fair and sweet and tender,
Dear brown-eyed little sweetheart mine,
As when, a callow youth and slender,
I asked to be your Valentine.

What though these years of ours be fleeting?
What though the years of youth be flown?
I'll mock old Tempus with repeating,
"I love my love and her alone!"

And when I fall before his reaping,
And when my stuttering speech is dumb,
Think not my love is dead or sleeping,
But that it waits for you to come.

So take, dear love, this little token,
And if there speaks in any line
The sentiment I'd fain have spoken,
Say, will you kiss your Valentine?

Eugene Field (1850-1895)

He Wishes for the Cloths of Heaven

Had I the heavens' embroidered cloths,
Enwrought with golden and silver light,
The blue and the dim and the dark cloths
Of night and light and the half-light,
I would spread the cloths under your feet:
But I, being poor, have only my dreams;
I have spread my dreams under your feet;
Tread softly because you tread on my dreams.

William Butler Yeats (1865-1939)

The Ragged Wood

O, hurry, where by water, among the trees,
The delicate-stepping stag and his lady sigh,
When they have looked upon their images
Would none had ever loved but you and I!

Or have you heard that sliding silver-shoed
Pale silver-proud queen-woman of the sky,
When the sun looked out of his golden hood?
O, that none ever loved but you and I!

O hurry to the ragged wood, for there
I will drive all those lovers out and cry
O, my share of the world, O, yellow hair!
No one has ever loved but you and I.

William Butler Yeats (1865-1939)

Ah, God, the way your little finger moved

Ah, God, the way your little finger moved
As you thrust a bare arm backward
And made play with your hair
And a comb a silly gilt comb
Ah, God—that I should suffer
Because of the way a little finger moved.

Stephen Crane (1871-1900)

Madonna of the Evening Flowers

All day long I have been working,
Now I am tired.
I call:"Where are you?"
But there is only the oak tree rustling in the wind.
The house is very quiet,
The sun shines in on your books,
On your scissors and thimble just put down,
But you are not there.
Suddenly I am lonely:
Where are you?
I go about searching.

Then I see you,
Standing under a spire of pale blue larkspur,
With a basket of roses on your arm.
You are cool, like silver,
And you smile.
I think the Canterbury bells are playing little tunes.

You tell me that the peonies need spraying,
That the columbines have overrun all bounds,
That the pyrus japonica should be cut back and rounded.
You tell me these things.
But I look at you, heart of silver,
White heart-flame of polished silver,
Burning beneath the blue steeples of the larkspur,
And I long to kneel instantly at your feet,
While all about us peal the loud,
sweet Te Deums of the Canterbury bells.

Amy Lowell (1874-1925)

I Love You

When April bends above me
And finds me fast asleep
Dust need not keep the secret
A live heart died to keep.

When April tells the thrushes,
The meadow-larks will know,
And pipe the three words lightly
To all the winds that blow.

Above his roof the swallows,
In notes like far-blown rain,
Will tell the little sparrow
Beside his window-pane.

O sparrow, little sparrow,
When I am fast asleep,
Then tell my love the secret
That I have died to keep.

Sara Teasdale (1884-1933)

Lovers

You were glad to-night: and now you've gone away.
Flushed in the dark, you put your dreams to bed;
But as you fall asleep I hear you say
Those tired sweet drowsy words we left unsaid.

Sleep well: for I can follow you, to bless
And lull your distant beauty where you roam;
And with wild songs of hoarded loveliness
Recall you to these arms that were your home.

Siegfried Sassoon (1886-1967)

Prelude

How could I love you more?
I would give up
Even that beauty I have loved too well
That I might love you better.
Alas, how poor the gifts that lovers give—
I can but give you of my flesh and strength,
I can but give you these few passing days
And passionate words that, since our speech began,
All lovers whisper in all ladies' ears.

I try to think of some one lovely gift
No lover yet in all the world has found;
I think: If the cold sombre gods
Were hot with love as I am
Could they not endow you with a star
And fix bright youth for ever in your limbs?
Could they not give you all things that I lack?

You should have loved a god; I am but dust.
Yet no god loves as loves this poor frail dust.

Richard Aldington (1892-1962)

Choice

I'd rather have the thought of you
To hold against my heart,
My spirit to be taught of you
With west winds blowing,
Than all the warm caresses
Of another love's bestowing,
Or all the glories of the world
In which you had no part.

I'd rather have the theme of you
To thread my nights and days,
I'd rather have the dream of you
With faint stars glowing,
I'd rather have the want of you,
The rich, elusive taunt of you
Forever and forever and forever unconfessed
Than claim the alien comfort
Of any other's breast.

O lover! O my lover,
That this should come to me!
I'd rather have the hope of you,
Ah, Love, I'd rather grope for you
Within the great abyss
Than claim another's kiss-
Alone I'd rather go my way
Throughout eternity.

Angela Morgan (1901-1957)

Poems About Desiring Love

The Looks of a Lover Enamoured

Thou, with thy looks, on whom I look full oft,
And find therein great cause of deep delight,
Thy face is fair, thy skin is smooth and soft,
Thy lips are sweet, thine eyes are clear and bright,
And every part seems pleasant in my sight;
Yet wote thou well, those looks have wrought my woe,
Because I love to look upon them so.

For first those looks allured mine eye to look,
And straight mine eye stirred up my heart to love;
And cruel love, with deep deceitful hook,
Choked up my mind, whom fancy cannot move,
Nor hope relieve, nor other help behoove
But still to look; and though I look too much,
Needs must I look because I see none such.

Thus in thy looks my love and life have hold;
And with such life my death draws on apace:
And for such death no med'cine can be told
But looking still upon thy lovely face,
Wherein are painted pity, peace, and grace.
Then though thy looks should cause me for to die,
Needs must I look, because I live thereby.

Since then thy looks my life have so in thrall
As I can like none other looks but thine,
Lo, here I yield my life, my love, and all
Into thy hands, and all things else resign
But liberty to gaze upon thine eyen:
Which when I do, then think it were thy part
To look again, and link with me in heart.

George Gasgione (1534-1577)

Phillis II

Love guards the roses of thy lips
And flies about them like a bee;
If I approach he forward skips,
And if I kiss he stingeth me.

Love in thine eyes doth build his bower,
And sleeps within their pretty shine;
And if I look the boy will lower,
And from their orbs shoot shafts divine.

Love works thy heart within his fire,
And in my tears doth firm the same;
And if I tempt it will retire,
And of my plaints doth make a game.

Love, let me cull her choicest flowers;
And pity me, and calm her eye;
Make soft her heart, dissolve her lowers
Then will I praise thy deity.

But if thou do not, Love, I'll truly serve her
In spite of thee, and by firm faith deserve her.

Thomas Lodge (1558-1625)

O Mistress Mine

O Mistress mine, where are you roaming?
O stay and hear! your true-love's coming
That can sing both high and low;
Trip no further, pretty sweeting,
Journeys end in lovers' meeting—
Every wise man's son doth know.

What is love? 'tis not hereafter;
Present mirth hath present laughter;
What's to come is still unsure:
In delay there lies no plenty,—
Then come kiss me, Sweet-and-twenty,
Youth's a stuff will not endure.

William Shakespeare (1564-1616)

A Valediction: Forbidding Mourning

As virtuous men pass mildly away,
And whisper to their souls to go,
Whilst some of their sad friends do say,
"The breath goes now," and some say, "No,"

So let us melt, and make no noise,
No tear-floods, nor sigh-tempests move;
'Twere profanation of our joys
To tell the laity our love.

Moving of the earth brings harms and fears,
Men reckon what it did and meant;
But trepidation of the spheres,
Though greater far, is innocent.

Dull sublunary lovers' love
(Whose soul is sense) cannot admit
Absence, because it doth remove
Those things which elemented it.

But we, by a love so much refined
That our selves know not what it is,
Inter-assured of the mind,
Care less, eyes, lips, and hands to miss.

Our two souls therefore, which are one,
Though I must go, endure not yet
A breach, but an expansion.
Like gold to airy thinness beat.

If they be two, they are two so
As stiff twin compasses are two:
Thy soul, the fixed foot, makes no show
To move, but doth, if the other do;

And though it in the center sit,
Yet when the other far doth roam,
It leans, and hearkens after it,
And grows erect, as that comes home.

Such wilt thou be to me, who must,
Like the other foot, obliquely run;
Thy firmness makes my circle just,
And makes me end where I begun.

John Donne (1572-1631)

The Bait

Come live with me, and be my love,
And we will some new pleasures prove
Of golden sands, and crystal brooks,
With silken lines and silver hooks.

There will the river whisp'ring run
Warm'd by thy eyes, more than the sun ;
And there th' enamour'd fish will stay,
Begging themselves they may betray.

When thou wilt swim in that live bath,
Each fish, which every channel hath,
Will amorously to thee swim,
Gladder to catch thee, than thou him.

If thou, to be so seen, be'st loth,
By sun or moon, thou dark'nest both,
And if myself have leave to see,
I need not their light, having thee.

Let others freeze with angling reeds,
And cut their legs with shells and weeds,
Or treacherously poor fish beset,
With strangling snare, or windowy net.

Let coarse bold hands from slimy nest
The bedded fish in banks out-wrest ;
Or curious traitors, sleeve-silk flies,
Bewitch poor fishes' wand'ring eyes.

For thee, thou need'st no such deceit,
For thou thyself art thine own bait :
That fish, that is not catch'd thereby,
Alas ! is wiser far than I.

John Donne (1572-1631)

Love Not Me

Love not me for comely grace,
For my pleasing eye or face;
Nor for any outward part,
No, nor for my constant heart:
For those may fail or turn to ill,
So thou and I shall sever.
Keep therefore a true woman's eye,
And love me still, but know not why;
So hast thou the same reason still
To doat upon me ever.

John Wilbye (1574-1638)

Go, lovely Rose

Go, lovely rose!
Tell her that wastes her time and me
That now she knows,
When I resemble her to thee,
How sweet and fair she seems to be.

Tell her that's young,
And shuns to have her graces spied,
That hadst thou sprung
In deserts, where no men abide,
Thou must have uncommended died.

Small is the worth
Of beauty from the light retired;
Bid her come forth,
Suffer herself to be desired,
And not blush so to be admired.

Then die! that she
The common fate of all things rare
May read in thee;
How small a part of time they share
That are so wondrous sweet and fair!

Edmund Waller (1606-1687)

To Mary

The twentieth year is well-nigh past,
Since first our sky was overcast;
Ah, would that this might be the last!
My Mary!
Thy spirits have a fainter flow,
I see thee daily weaker grow--
'Twas my distress that brought thee low,
My Mary!
Thy needles, once a shining store,
For my sake restless heretofore,
No rust disused, and shine no more,
My Mary!
For though thou gladly wouldst fulfil
The same kind office for me still,
Thy sight now seconds not thy will,
My Mary!
But well thou play'd the housewife's part,
And all thy threads with magic art
Have wound themselves about this heart,
My Mary!
Thy indistinct expressions seem
Like language utter'd in a dream;
Yet me they charm, whate'er the theme,
My Mary!
Thy silver locks, once auburn bright,
Are still more lovely in my sight
Than golden beams of orient light,
My Mary!
For could I view nor them nor thee,
What sight worth seeing could I see?
The sun would rise in vain for me,
My Mary!
Partakers of thy sad decline,
Thy hands their little force resign;
Yet, gently press'd, press gently mine,
My Mary!
And then I feel that still I hold
A richer store ten thousandfold
Than misers fancy in their gold,

My Mary!
Such feebleness of limbs thou prov'st,
That now at every step thou mov'st
Upheld by two; yet still thou lov'st,
My Mary!
And still to love, though press'd with ill,
In wintry age to feel no chill,
With me is to be lovely still,
My Mary!
But ah! by constant heed I know
How oft the sadness that I show
Transforms thy smiles to looks of woe,
My Mary!
And should my future lot be cast
With much resemblance of the past,
Thy worn-out heart will break at last,
My Mary!

William Cowper (1731-1800)

The Garden of Love

I laid me down upon a bank,
Where Love lay sleeping;
I heard among the rushes dank
Weeping, weeping.
Then I went to the heath and the wild,
To the thistles and thorns of the waste;
And they told me how they were beguiled,
Driven out, and compelled to the chaste.
I went to the Garden of Love,
And saw what I never had seen;
A Chapel was built in the midst,
Where I used to play on the green.
And the gates of this Chapel were shut
And "Thou shalt not," writ over the door;
So I turned to the Garden of Love
That so many sweet flowers bore.
And I saw it was filled with graves,
And tombstones where flowers should be;
And priests in black gowns were walking their rounds,
And binding with briars my joys and desires.

William Blake (1757-1827)

Valentine Song

Dearest, let these roses
In their purity,
Be a present symbol
Of my love for thee.
Underneath the blossom
Thorns are sure to grow;
Take heed lest you touch them,
They would pain you so!
Ah! my faults like thorns are,
But cannot they be
Hidden 'neath the flower
Of my love for thee?

Robert Argyle Campbell (1769-1846)

An Argument

I've oft been told by learned friars,
That wishing and the crime are one,
And Heaven punishes desires
As much as if the deed were done.

If wishing damns us, you and I
Are damned to all our heart's content;
Come, then, at least we may enjoy
Some pleasure for our punishment!

Thomas Moore (1779-1852)

To Harriet

Whose is the love that, gleaming through the world,
   Wards off the poisonous arrow of its scorn?
   Whose is the warm and partial praise,
     Virtue's most sweet reward?

Beneath whose looks did my reviving soul
   Riper in truth and virtuous daring grow?
   Whose eyes have I gazed fondly on,
     And loved mankind the more?

Harriet! on thine:—thou wert my purer mind;
   Thou wert the inspiration of my song;
   Thine are these early wilding flowers,
     Though garlanded by me.

Then press into thy breast this pledge of love;
And know, though time may change and years may roll,
   Each floweret gathered in my heart
     It consecrates to thine.

Percy Bysshe Shelley (1792-1822)

Love's Philosophy

The fountains mingle with the river
And the rivers with the ocean,
The winds of heaven mix for ever
With a sweet emotion;
Nothing in the world is single,
All things by a law divine
In one another's being mingle—
Why not I with thine?

See the mountains kiss high heaven,
And the waves clasp one another;
No sister-flower would be forgiven
If it disdain'd its brother;
And the sunlight clasps the earth,
And the moonbeams kiss the sea—
What are all these kissings worth,
If thou kiss not me?

Percy Bysshe Shelley (1792-1822)

To Mary

I sleep with thee, and wake with thee,
    And yet thou art not there;
I fill my arms with thoughts of thee,
    And press the common air.
Thy eyes are gazing upon mine
    When thou art out of sight;
My lips are always touching thine
    At morning, noon, and night.

I think and speak of other things
    To keep my mind at rest,
But still to thee my memory clings
    Like love in woman's breast.
I hide it from the world's wide eye
    And think and speak contrary,
But soft the wind comes from the sky
    And whispers tales of Mary.

The night-wind whispers in my ear,
    The moon shines on my face;
The burden still of chilling fear
    I find in every place.
The breeze is whispering in the bush,
    And the leaves fall from the tree,
All sighing on, and will not hush,
    Some pleasant tales of thee.

John Clare (1793-1864)

Secret Love

I hid my love when young till I
Couldn't bear the buzzing of a fly;
I hid my love to my despite
Till I could not bear to look at light:
I dare not gaze upon her face
But left her memory in each place;
Where eer I saw a wild flower lie
I kissed and bade my love good bye.
I met her in the greenest dells
Where dewdrops pearl the wood blue bells
The lost breeze kissed her bright blue eye,
The bee kissed and went singing by,
A sunbeam found a passage there,
A gold chain round her neck so fair;
As secret as the wild bee's song
She lay there all the summer long.
I hid my love in field and town
Till een the breeze would knock me down,
The bees seemed singing ballads oer,
The fly's bass turned a lion's roar;
And even silence found a tongue,
To haunt me all the summer long;
The riddle nature could not prove
Was nothing else but secret love.

John Clare (1793-1864)

To Mary: I Sleep with Thee

I sleep with thee, and wake with thee,
    And yet thou art not there;
I fill my arms with thoughts of thee,
    And press the common air.
Thy eyes are gazing upon mine
    When thou art out of sight;
My lips are always touching thine
    At morning, noon, and night.
I think and speak of other things
    To keep my mind at rest,
But still to thee my memory clings
    Like love in woman's breast.
I hide it from the world's wide eye
    And think and speak contrary,
But soft the wind comes from the sky
    And whispers tales of Mary.
The night-wind whispers in my ear,
    The moon shines on my face;
The burden still of chilling fear
    I find in every place.
The breeze is whispering in the bush,
    And the leaves fall from the tree,
All sighing on, and will not hush,
    Some pleasant tales of thee.

John Clare (1793-1864)

In Three Days

So, I shall see her in three days
And just one night, but nights are short,
Then two long hours, and that is morn.
See how I come, unchanged, unworn!
Feel, where my life broke off from thine,
How fresh the splinters keep and fine---
Only a touch and we combine!

Too long, this time of year, the days!
But nights, at least the nights are short.
As night shows where ger one moon is,
A hand's-breadth of pure light and bliss,
So life's night gives my lady birth
And my eyes hold her! What is worth
The rest of heaven, the rest of earth?

O loaded curls, release your store
Of warmth and scent, as once before
The tingling hair did, lights and darks
Outbreaking into fairy sparks,
When under curl and curl I pried
After the warmth and scent inside,
Thro' lights and darks how manifold---
The dark inspired, the light controlled
As early Art embrowns the gold.

What great fear, should one say, "Three days
"That change the world might change as well
"Your fortune; and if joy delays,
"Be happy that no worse befell!"
What small fear, if another says,
"Three days and one short night beside
"May throw no shadow on your ways;
"But years must teem with change untried,
"With chance not easily defied,
"With an end somewhere undescried."
No fear!---or if a fear be born
This minute, it dies out in scorn.
Fear? I shall see her in three days

And one night, now the nights are short,
Then just two hours, and that is morn.

Robert Browning (1812-1889)

Two in the Campagna

I wonder do you feel today
As I have felt since, hand in hand,
We sat down on the grass, to stray
In spirit better through the land,
This morn of Rome and May?

For me, I touched a thought, I know,
Has tantalized mc many times,
(Like turns of thread the spiders throw
Mocking across our path) for rhymes
To catch at and let go.

Help me to hold it! First it left
The yellowing fennel, run to seed
There, branching from the brickwork's cleft,
Some old tomb's ruin: yonder weed
Took up the floating weft,

Where one small orange cup amassed
Five beetles—blind and green they grope
Among the honey-meal: and last,
Everywhere on the grassy slope
I traced it. Hold it fast!

The champaign with its endless fleece
Of feathery grasses everywhere!
Silence and passion, joy and peace,
An everlasting wash of air—
Rome's ghost since her decease.

Such life here, through such lengths of hours,
Such miracles performed in play,
Such primal naked forms of flowers,
Such letting nature have her way
While heaven looks from its towers!

How say you? Let us, O my dove,
Let us be unashamed of soul,
As earth lies bare to heaven above!

How is it under our control
To love or not to love?

I would that you were all to me,
You that are just so much, no more.
Nor yours nor mine, nor slave nor free!
Where does the fault lie? What the core
O' the wound, since wound must be?

I would I could adopt your will,
See with your eyes, and set my heart
Beating by yours, and drink my fill
At your soul's springs—your part my part
In life, for good and ill.

No. I yearn upward, touch you close,
Then stand away. I kiss your cheek,
Catch your soul's warmth—I pluck the rose
And love it more than tongue can speak—
Then the good minute goes.

Already how am I so far
Out of that minute? Must I go
Still like the thistle-ball, no bar,
Onward, whenever light winds blow,
Fixed by no friendly star?

Just when I seemed about to learn!
Where is the thread now? Off again!
The old trick! Only I discern—
Infinite passion, and the pain
Of finite hearts that yearn.

Robert Browning (1812-1889)

If Grief for Grief can Touch Thee

If grief for grief can touch thee,
If answering woe for woe,
If any truth can melt thee
Come to me now!

I cannot be more lonely,
More drear I cannot be!
My worn heart beats so wildly
'Twill break for thee--

And when the world despises--
When Heaven repels my prayer--
Will not mine angel comfort?
Mine idol hear?

Yes, by the tears I'm poured,
By all my hours of pain
O I shall surely win thee,
Beloved, again!

Emily Bronte (1818-1848)

Longing

Come to me in my dreams, and then
By day I shall be well again!
For then the night will more than pay
The hopeless longing of the day.

Come, as thou cam'st a thousand times,
A messenger from radiant climes,
And smile on thy new world, and be
As kind to others as to me!

Or, as thou never cam'st in sooth,
Come now, and let me dream it truth;
And part my hair, and kiss my brow,
And say: *My love! why sufferest thou?*

Come to me in my dreams, and then
By day I shall be well again!
For then the night will more than pay
The hopeless longing of the day.

Matthew Arnold (1822-1888)

A charm invests a face

A charm invests a face
Imperfectly beheld.
The lady dare not lift her veil
For fear it be dispelled.

But peers beyond her mesh,
And wishes, and denies,
'Lest interview annul a want
That image satisfies.

Emily Dickinson (1830-1886)

Silentium Amoris

As often-times the too resplendent sun
Hurries the pallid and reluctant moon
Back to her sombre cave, ere she hath won
A single ballad from the nightingale,
So doth thy Beauty make my lips to fail,
And all my sweetest singing out of tune.

And as at dawn across the level mead
On wings impetuous some wind will come,
And with its too harsh kisses break the reed
Which was its only instrument of song,
So my too stormy passions work me wrong,
And for excess of Love my Love is dumb.

But surely unto Thee mine eyes did show
Why I am silent, and my lute unstrung;
Else it were better we should part, and go,
Thou to some lips of sweeter melody,
And I to nurse the barren memory
Of unkissed kisses, and songs never sung.

Oscar Wilde (1854-1900)

If I Were Her Lover

I

If I were her lover,
I'd wade through the clover
Over the fields before
The gate that leads to her door;
Over the meadows,
To wait, 'mid the shadows,
The shadows that circle her door,
For the heart of my heart and more.
And there in the clover
Close by her,
Over and over
I'd sigh her:
"Your eyes are as brown
As the Night's, looking down
On waters that sleep
With the moon in their deep" . . .
If I were her lover to sigh her.

II

If I were her lover,
I'd wade through the clover
Over the fields before
The lane that leads to her door;
I'd wait, 'mid the thickets,
Or there by the pickets,
White pickets that fence in her door,
For the life of my life and more.
I'd lean in the clover—
The crisper
For the dews that are over—
And whisper:
"Your lips are as rare
As the dewberries there,
As ripe and as red,
On the honey-dew fed" . . .
If I were her lover to whisper.

III

If I were her lover,
I'd wade through the clover
Over the field before
The pathway that leads to her door;
And watch, in the twinkle
Of stars that sprinkle
The paradise over her door,
For the soul of my soul and more.
And there in the clover
I'd reach her;
And over and over
I'd teach her—
A love without sighs,
Of laughterful eyes,
That reckoned each second
The pause of a kiss,
A kiss and . . . that is
If I were her lover to teach her.

Madison Julius Cawein (1865-1914)

A Dream Girl

You will come one day in a waver of love,
Tender as dew, impetuous as rain,
The tan of the sun will be on your skin,
The purr of the breeze in your murmuring speech,
You will pose with a hill-flower grace.

You will come, with your slim, expressive arms,
A poise of the head no sculptor has caught
And nuances spoken with shoulder and neck,
Your face in pass-and-repass of moods
As many as skies in delicate change
Of cloud and blue and flimmering sun.

Yet,
You may not come, O girl of a dream,
We may but pass as the world goes by
And take from a look of eyes into eyes,
A film of hope and a memoried day.

Carl Sandburg (1878-1967)

I Would Live in Your Love

I would live in your love as the sea-grasses live in the sea,
Borne up by each wave as it passes, drawn down by each wave that
recedes;

I would empty my soul of the dreams that have gathered in me,
I would beat with your heart as it beats, I would follow your soul
as it leads.

Sara Teasdale (1884-1933)

Love Me

Brown-thrush singing all day long
In the leaves above me,
Take my love this April song,
"Love me, love me, love me!"

When he harkens what you say,
Bid him, lest he miss me,
Leave his work or leave his play,
And kiss me, kiss me, kiss me!

Sara Teasdale (1884-1933)

Poems About Power of Love

Ah, My Beloved

Ah, my beloved, fill the cup that clears
Today of past regrets and future fears;
Tomorrow? Why, tomorrow I may be,
Myself, with yesterday's sev'n thousand years.

Omar Khayyam (1048-1131)

Sonnet 30

My love is like to ice, and I to fire:
How comes it then that this her cold is so great
Is not dissolved through my so hot desire,
But harder grows the more I her entreat?
Or how comes it that my exceeding heat
Is not allayed by her heart frozen cold,
But that I burn much more in boiling sweat,
And feel my flames augmented manifold?
What more miraculous thing may be told,
That fire which all things melts should harden ice:
And ice which is congealed with senseless cold,
Should kindle fire by wonderful device?
Such is the power of love in gentle mind,
That it can alter all the course of kind.

Edmund Spenser (1552-1599)

My Love is Like to Ice

My love is like to ice, and I to fire:
How come it then that this her cold is so great
Is not dissolved through my so hot desire,
But harder grows the more I her entreat?
Or how comes it that my exceeding heat
Is not allayed by her heart-frozen cold,
But that I burn much more in boiling sweat,
And feel my flames augmented manifold?
What more miraculous thing may be told,
That fire, which is congealed with senseless cold,
Should kindle fire by wonderful device?
Such is the power of love in gentle mind,
That it can alter all the course of kind.

Edmund Spenser (1552-1599)

Love is a Sickness

Love is a sickness full of woes,
All remedies refusing;
A plant that with most cutting grows,
Most barren with best using.
Why so?

More we enjoy it, more it dies;
If not enjoy'd, it sighing cries--
Heigh ho!

Love is a torment of the mind,
A tempest everlasting;
And Jove hath made it of a kind
Not well, nor full nor fasting.
Why so?

More we enjoy it, more it dies;
If not enjoy'd, it sighing cries--
Heigh ho!

Samuel Daniel (1562-1619)

Sonnet 46

Mine eye and heart are at a mortal war,
How to divide the conquest of thy sight;
Mine eye my heart thy picture's sight would bar,
My heart mine eye the freedom of that right.
My heart doth plead that thou in him dost lie,
A closet never pierc'd with crystal eyes
But the defendant doth that plea deny,
And says in him thy fair appearance lies.
To side this title is impannelled
A quest of thoughts, all tenants to the heart;
And by their verdict is determined
The clear eye's moiety, and the dear heart's part:
As thus; mine eye's due is thy outward part,
And my heart's right, thy inward love of heart.

William Shakespeare (1564-1616)

Sonnet 141

In faith I do not love thee with mine eyes,
For they in thee a thousand errors note;
But 'tis my heart that loves what they despise,
Who, in despite of view, is pleased to dote.
Nor are mine ears with thy tongue's tune delighted;
Nor tender feeling, to base touches prone,
Nor taste, nor smell, desire to be invited
To any sensual feast with thee alone:
But my five wits nor my five senses can
Dissuade one foolish heart from serving thee,
Who leaves unsway'd the likeness of a man,
Thy proud heart's slave and vassal wretch to be:
Only my plague thus far I count my gain,
That she that makes me sin awards me pain.

William Shakespeare (1564-1616)

Sonnet 153

Cupid laid by his brand and fell asleep:
A maid of Dian's this advantage found,
And his love-kindling fire did quickly steep
In a cold valley-fountain of that ground;
Which borrow'd from this holy fire of Love,
A dateless lively heat, still to endure,
And grew a seeting bath, which yet men prove
Against strange maladies a sovereign cure.
But at my mistress' eye Love's brand new-fired,
The boy for trial needs would touch my breast;
I, sick withal, the help of bath desired,
And thither hied, a sad distemper'd guest,
But found no cure, the bath for my help lies
Where Cupid got new fire; my mistress' eyes.

William Shakespeare (1564-1616)

Who Ever Loved, That Loved Not at First Sight?

It lies not in our power to love or hate,
For will in us is overruled by fate.
When two are stripped, long ere the course begin,
We wish that one should love, the other win;
And one especially do we affect
Of two gold ingots, like in each respect:
The reason no man knows, let it suffice,
What we behold is censured by our eyes.
Where both deliberate, the love is slight:
Who ever loved, that loved not at first sight?

Christopher Marlowe (1564-1593)

The Sun Rising

Busy old fool, unruly Sun,
Why dost thou thus,
Through windows, and through curtains, call on us?
Must to thy motions lovers' seasons run?
Saucy pedantic wretch, go chide
Late school-boys and sour prentices,
Go tell court-huntsmen that the king will ride,
Call country ants to harvest offices;
Love, all alike, no season knows nor clime,
Nor hours, days, months, which are the rags of time.
Thy beams so reverend, and strong
Why shouldst thou think?
I could eclipse and cloud them with a wink,
But that I would not lose her sight so long.
If her eyes have not blinded thine,
Look, and to-morrow late tell me,
Whether both th' Indias of spice and mine
Be where thou left'st them, or lie here with me.
Ask for those kings whom thou saw'st yesterday,
And thou shalt hear, "All here in one bed lay."
She's all states, and all princes I;
Nothing else is;
Princes do but play us ; compared to this,
All honour's mimic, all wealth alchemy.
Thou, Sun, art half as happy as we,
In that the world's contracted thus;
Thine age asks ease, and since thy duties be
To warm the world, that's done in warming us.
Shine here to us, and thou art everywhere;
This bed thy center is, these walls thy sphere.

John Donne (1572-1631)

The Ecstasy

Where, like a pillow on a bed,
A pregnant bank swell'd up, to rest
The violet's reclining head,
Sat we two, one another's best.

Our hands were firmly cemented
By a fast balm, which thence did spring;
Our eye-beams twisted, and did thread
Our eyes upon one double string.

So to engraft our hands, as yet
Was all the means to make us one;
And pictures in our eyes to get
Was all our propagation.

As, 'twixt two equal armies, Fate
Suspends uncertain victory,
Our souls—which to advance their state,
Were gone out—hung 'twixt her and me.

And whilst our souls negotiate there,
We like sepulchral statues lay;
All day, the same our postures were,
And we said nothing, all the day.

If any, so by love refined,
That he soul's language understood,
And by good love were grown all mind,
Within convenient distance stood,

He—though he knew not which soul spake,
Because both meant, both spake the same—
Might thence a new concoction take,
And part far purer than he came.

This ecstasy doth unperplex
(We said) and tell us what we love;
We see by this, it was not sex;
We see, we saw not, what did move:

But as all several souls contain
Mixture of things they know not what,
Love these mix'd souls doth mix again,
And makes both one, each this, and that.

A single violet transplant,
The strength, the colour, and the size—
All which before was poor and scant—
Redoubles still, and multiplies.

When love with one another so
Interanimates two souls,
That abler soul, which thence doth flow,
Defects of loneliness controls.

We then, who are this new soul, know,
Of what we are composed, and made,
For th' atomies of which we grow
Are souls, whom no change can invade.

But, O alas ! so long, so far,
Our bodies why do we forbear?
They are ours, though not we; we are
Th' intelligences, they the spheres.

We owe them thanks, because they thus
Did us, to us, at first convey,
Yielded their senses' force to us,
Nor are dross to us, but allay.

On man heaven's influence works not so,
But that it first imprints the air;
For soul into the soul may flow,
Though it to body first repair.

As our blood labours to beget
Spirits, as like souls as it can;
Because such fingers need to knit
That subtle knot, which makes us man;

So must pure lovers' souls descend
To affections, and to faculties,
Which sense may reach and apprehend,
Else a great prince in prison lies.

To our bodies turn we then, that so
Weak men on love reveal'd may look;
Love's mysteries in souls do grow,
But yet the body is his book.

And if some lover, such as we,
Have heard this dialogue of one,
Let him still mark us, he shall see
Small change when we're to bodies gone.

John Donne (1572-1631)

Batter My Heart

Batter my heart, three person'd God; for, you
As yet but knock, breathe, shine, and seek to mend;
That I may rise, and stand, o'erthrow me, and bend
Your force, to break, blow, burn and make me new.
I, like an usurpt town, to another due,
Labour to admit you, but Oh, to no end,
Reason, your viceroy in me, me should defend,
But is captiv'd, and proves weak or untrue,
Yet dearly I love you, and would be lov'd faine,
But am betroth'd unto your enemy,
Divorce me, untie, or break that knot again,
Take me to you, imprison me, for I
Except you enthrall me, never shall be free,
Nor ever chast, except you ravish me.

John Donne (1572-1631)

Tell Me No More

Tell me no more how fair she is,
I have no minde to hear
The story of that distant bliss
I never shall come near:
By sad experience I have found
That her perfection is my wound.
And tell me not how fond I am
To tempt a daring Fate,
From whence no triumph ever came,
But to repent too late:
There is some hope ere long I may
In silence dote my self away.
I ask no pity (Love) from thee,
Nor will thy justice blame,
So that thou wilt not envy mee
The glory of my flame:
Which crowns my heart when ere it dyes,
In that it falls her sacrifice.

Henry King (1592-1669)

When, Dearest, I but Think of Thee

When, dearest, I but think of thee,
Methinks all things that lovely be
Are present, and my soul delighted:
For beauties that from worth arise
Are like the grace of deities,
Still present with us, tho' unsighted.

Thus while I sit and sigh the day
With all his borrow'd lights away,
Till night's black wings do overtake me,
Thinking on thee, thy beauties then,
As sudden lights do sleepy men,
So they by their bright rays awake me.

Thus absence dies, and dying proves
No absence can subsist with loves
That do partake of fair perfection:
Since in the darkest night they may
By love's quick motion find a way
To see each other by reflection.

The waving sea can with each flood
Bathe some high promont that hath stood
Far from the main up in the river:
O think not then but love can do
As much! for that 's an ocean too,
Which flows not every day, but ever!

Sir John Suckling (1609-1642)

Tell Me Not, Sweet, I am Unkind

Tell me not, Sweet, I am unkind
For, from the nunnery
Of thy chaste breast, and quiet mind,
To war and arms I fly.

True, a new mistress now I chase,
The first foe in the field;
And with a stronger faith- embrace
A sword, a horse, a shield.

Yet this unconstancy is such
As you too shall adore;
For, I could not love thee, Dear, so much,
Loved I not honour more.

Richard Lovelace (1618-1657)

Lochinvar

OH! young Lochinvar is come out of the west,
Through all the wide Border his steed was the best;
And save his good broadsword he weapons had none.
He rode all unarmed and he rode all alone.
So faithful in love and so dauntless in war,
There never was knight like the young Lochinvar.
He stayed not for brake and he stopped not for stone,
He swam the Eske river where ford there was none,
But ere he alighted at Netherby gate
The bride had consented, the gallant came late:
For a laggard in love and a dastard in war
Was to wed the fair Ellen of brave Lochinvar.
So boldly he entered the Netherby Hall,
Among bridesmen, and kinsmen, and brothers, and all:
Then spoke the bride's father, his hand on his sword,--
For the poor craven bridegroom said never a word,--
'Oh! come ye in peace here, or come ye in war,
Or to dance at our bridal, young Lord Lochinvar?'--
'I long wooed your daughter, my suit you denied;
Love swells like the Solway, but ebbs like its tide--
And now am I come, with this lost love of mine,
To lead but one measure, drink one cup of wine.
There are maidens in Scotland more lovely by far,
That would gladly be bride to the young Lochinvar.'
The bride kissed the goblet; the knight took it up,
He quaffed off the wine, and he threw down the cup,
She looked down to blush, and she looked up to sigh,
With a smile on her lips and a tear in her eye.
He took her soft hand ere her mother could bar,--
'Now tread we a measure!' said young Lochinvar.
So stately his form, and so lovely her face,
That never a hall such a galliard did grace;
While her mother did fret, and her father did fume,
And the bridegroom stood dangling his bonnet and plume;
And the bride -- maidens whispered "Twere better by far
To have matched our fair cousin with young Lochinvar.'
One touch to her hand and one word in her ear,
When they reached the hall-door, and the charger stood near;
So light to the croupe the fair lady he swung,

So light to the saddle before her he sprung!
'She is won! we are gone, over bank, bush, and scaur;
They'll have fleet steeds that follow,' quoth young Lochinvar.
There was mounting 'mong Graemes of the Netherby clan;
Fosters, Fenwicks, and Musgraves, they rode and they ran:
There was racing and chasing on Cannobie Lee,
But the lost bride of Netherby ne'er did they see.
So daring in love and so dauntless in war,
Have ye e'er heard of gallant like young Lochinvar?

Sir Walter Scott (1771-1832)

Freedom and Love

How delicious is the winning
Of a kiss at love's beginning,
When two mutual hearts are sighing
For the knot there's no untying!
Yet remember, 'Midst our wooing,
Love has bliss, but Love has ruing;
Other smiles may make you fickle,
Tears for other charms may trickle.
Love he comes, and Love he tarries,
Just as fate or fancy carries;
Longest stays, when sorest chidden;
Laughs and flies, when press'd and bidden.
Bind the sea to slumber stilly,
Bind its odour to the lily,
Bind the aspen ne'er to quiver,
Then bind Love to last for ever.
Love's a fire that needs renewal
Of fresh beauty for its fuel:
Love's wing moults when caged and captured,
Only free, he soars enraptured.
Can you keep the bee from ranging
Or the ringdove's neck from changing?
No! nor fetter'd Love from dying
In the knot there's no untying.

Thomas Campbell (1777-1844)

Of Pearls and Stars

The pearly treasures of the sea,
The lights that spatter heaven above,
More precious than these wonders are
My heart-of-hearts filled with your love.

The ocean's power, the heavenly sights
Cannot outweigh a love filled heart.
And sparkling stars or glowing pearls
Pale as love flashes, beams and darts.

So, little, youthful maiden come
Into my ample, feverish heart
For heaven and earth and sea and sky
Do melt as love has melt my heart.

Heinrich Heine (1797-1856)

Give All to Love

Give all to love;
Obey thy heart;
Friends, kindred, days,
Estate, good-fame,
Plans, credit, and the Muse,—
Nothing refuse.

'Tis a brave master;
Let it have scope:
Follow it utterly,
Hope beyond hope:
High and more high
It dives into noon,
With wing unspent,
Untold intent;
But it is a God,
Knows its own path
And the outlets of the sky.

It was never for the mean;
It requireth courage stout.
Souls above doubt,
Valor unbending,
It will reward,—
They shall return
More than they were,
And ever ascending.

Leave all for love;
Yet, hear me, yet,
One word more thy heart behoved,
One pulse more of firm endeavor,—
Keep thee to-day,
To-morrow, forever,
Free as an Arab
Of thy beloved.

Cling with life to the maid;
But when the surprise,

First vague shadow of surmise
Flits across her bosom young,
Of a joy apart from thee,
Free be she, fancy-free;
Nor thou detain her vesture's hem,
Nor the palest rose she flung
From her summer diadem.

Though thou loved her as thyself,
As a self of purer clay,
Though her parting dims the day,
Stealing grace from all alive;
Heartily know,
When half-gods go,
The gods survive.

Ralph Waldo Emerson (1803-1882)

I Thought Once How Theocritus Had Sung

I thought once how Theocritus had sung
Of the sweet years, the dear and wished-for years,
Who each one in a gracious hand appears
To bear a gift for mortals, old or young:
And, as I mused it in his antique tongue,
I saw, in gradual vision through my tears,
The sweet, sad years, the melancholy years,
Those of my own life, who by turns had flung
A shadow across me. Straightway I was 'ware,
So weeping, how a mystic Shape did move
Behind me, and drew me backward by the hair;
And a voice said in mastery, while I strove,—
"Guess now who holds thee!"—"Death," I said, But, there,
The silver answer rang, "Not Death, but Love."

Elizabeth Barrett Browning (1806-1861)

Love Not

Love not, love not! ye hapless sons of clay!
Hope's gayest wreaths are made of earthly flowers—
Things that are made to fade and fall away
Ere they have blossom'd for a few short hours.
Love not!

Love not! the thing ye love may change:
The rosy lip may cease to smile on you,
The kindly-beaming eye grow cold and strange,
The heart still warmly beat, yet not be true.
Love not!

Love not! the thing you love may die,
May perish from the gay and gladsome earth;
The silent stars, the blue and smiling sky,
Beam o'er its grave, as once upon its birth.
Love not!

Love not! oh warning vainly said
In present hours as in the years gone by;
Love flings a halo round the dear ones' head,
Faultless, immortal, till they change or die,
Love not!

Caroline Elizabeth Sarah Norton (1808-1877)

A Woman's Last Word

Let's contend no more, Love,
Strive nor weep:
All be as before, Love,
---Only sleep!

What so wild as words are?
I and thou
In debate, as birds are,
Hawk on bough!

See the creature stalking
While we speak!
Hush and hide the talking,
Cheek on cheek!

What so false as truth is,
False to thee?
Where the serpent's tooth is
Shun the tree—

Where the apple reddens
Never pry---
Lest we lose our Edens,
Eve and I.

Be a god and hold me
With a charm!
Be a man and fold me
With thine arm!

Teach me, only teach, Love
As I ought
I will speak thy speech, Love,
Think thy thought—

Meet, if thou require it,
Both demands,
Laying flesh and spirit
In thy hands.

That shall be to-morrow
Not to-night:
I must bury sorrow
Out of sight:

--Must a little weep, Love,
(Foolish me!)
And so fall asleep, Love,
Loved by thee.

Robert Browning (1812-1889)

Cristina

She should never have looked at me
If she meant I should not love her!
There are plenty ... men, you call such,
I suppose ... she may discover
All her soul to, if she pleases,
And yet leave much as she found them:
But I'm not so, and she knew it
When she fixed me, glancing round them,

What? To fix me thus meant nothing?
But I can't tell (there's my weakness)
What her look said!---no vile cant, sure,
About ``need to strew the bleakness
``Of some lone shore with its pearl-seed.
``That the sea feels''---no strange yearning
``That such souls have, most to lavish
``Where there's chance of least returning.''

Oh, we're sunk enough here, God knows!
But not quite so sunk that moments,
Sure tho' seldom, are denied us,
When the spirit's true endowments
Stand out plainly from its false ones,
And apprise it if pursuing
Or the right way or the wrong way,
To its triumph or undoing.

There are flashes struck from midnights,
There are fire-flames noondays kindle,
Whereby piled-up honours perish,
Whereby swollen ambitions dwindle,
While just this or that poor impulse,
Which for once had play unstifled,
Seems the sole work of a life-time
That away the rest have trifled.

Doubt you if, in some such moment,
As she fixed me, she felt clearly,
Ages past the soul existed,

Here an age 'tis resting merely,
And hence fleets again for ages,
While the true end, sole and single,
It stops here for is, this love-way,
With some other soul to mingle?

Else it loses what it lived for,
And eternally must lose it;
Better ends may be in prospect,
Deeper blisses (if you choose it),
But this life's end and this love-bliss
Have been lost here. Doubt you whether
This she felt as, looking at me,
Mine and her souls rushed together?

Oh, observe! Of course, next moment,
The world's honours, in derision,
Trampled out the light for ever:
Never fear but there's provision
Of the devil's to quench knowledge
Lest we walk the earth in rapture!
---Making those who catch God's secret
Just so much more prize their capture!

Such am I: the secret's mine now!
She has lost me, I have gained her;
Her soul's mine: and thus, grown perfect,
I shall pass my life's remainder.
Life will just hold out the proving
Both our powers, alone and blended:
And then, come next life quickly!
This world's use will have been ended.

Robert Browning (1812-1889)

The Last Ride Together

I said--Then, dearest, since 'tis so,
Since now at length my fate I know,
Since nothing all my love avails,
Since all, my life seem'd meant for, fails,
Since this was written and needs must be--
My whole heart rises up to bless
Your name in pride and thankfulness!
Take back the hope you gave,--I claim
Only a memory of the same,
--And this beside, if you will not blame;
Your leave for one more last ride with me.

My mistress bent that brow of hers,
Those deep dark eyes where pride demurs
When pity would be softening through,
Fix'd me a breathing-while or two
With life or death in the balance: right!
The blood replenish'd me again;
My last thought was at least not vain:
I and my mistress, side by side
Shall be together, breathe and ride,
So, one day more am I deified.
Who knows but the world may end to-night?

Hush! if you saw some western cloud
All billowy-bosom'd, over-bow'd
By many benedictions--sun's
And moon's and evening-star's at once--
And so, you, looking and loving best,
Conscious grew, your passion drew
Cloud, sunset, moonrise, star-shine too,
Down on you, near and yet more near,
Till flesh must fade for heaven was here!--
Thus leant she and linger'd--joy and fear!
Thus lay she a moment on my breast.

Then we began to ride. My soul
Smooth'd itself out, a long-cramp'd scroll
Freshening and fluttering in the wind.

Past hopes already lay behind.
What need to strive with a life awry?
Had I said that, had I done this,
So might I gain, so might I miss.
Might she have loved me? just as well
She might have hated, who can tell!
Where had I been now if the worst befell?
And here we are riding, she and I.

Fail I alone, in words and deeds?
Why, all men strive and who succeeds?
We rode; it seem'd my spirit flew,
Saw other regions, cities new,
As the world rush'd by on either side.
I thought,--All labour, yet no less
Bear up beneath their unsuccess.
Look at the end of work, contrast
The petty done, the undone vast,
This present of theirs with the hopeful past!
I hoped she would love me; here we ride.

What hand and brain went ever pair'd?
What heart alike conceived and dared?
What act proved all its thought had been?
What will but felt the fleshly screen?
We ride and I see her bosom heave.
There's many a crown for who can reach.
Ten lines, a statesman's life in each!
The flag stuck on a heap of bones,
A soldier's doing! what atones?
They scratch his name on the Abbey-stones.
My riding is better, by their leave.

What does it all mean, poet? Well,
Your brains beat into rhythm, you tell
What we felt only; you express'd
You hold things beautiful the best,
And pace them in rhyme so, side by side.
'Tis something, nay 'tis much: but then,
Have you yourself what's best for men?
Are you--poor, sick, old ere your time--
Nearer one whit your own sublime
Than we who never have turn'd a rhyme?
Sing, riding's a joy! For me, I ride.

And you, great sculptor--so, you gave
A score of years to Art, her slave,
And that's your Venus, whence we turn
To yonder girl that fords the burn!
You acquiesce, and shall I repine?
What, man of music, you grown gray
With notes and nothing else to say,
Is this your sole praise from a friend?--
'Greatly his opera's strains intend,
But in music we know how fashions end!'
I gave my youth: but we ride, in fine.

Who knows what's fit for us? Had fate
Proposed bliss here should sublimate
My being--had I sign'd the bond--
Still one must lead some life beyond,
Have a bliss to die with, dim-descried.
This foot once planted on the goal,
This glory-garland round my soul,
Could I descry such? Try and test!
I sink back shuddering from the quest.
Earth being so good, would heaven seem best?
Now, heaven and she are beyond this ride.

And yet--she has not spoke so long!
What if heaven be that, fair and strong
At life's best, with our eyes upturn'd
Whither life's flower is first discern'd,
We, fix'd so, ever should so abide?
What if we still ride on, we two
With life for ever old yet new,
Changed not in kind but in degree,
The instant made eternity,--
And heaven just prove that I and she
Ride, ride together, for ever ride?

Robert Browning (1812-1889)

I loved her for that she was beautiful

I loved her for that she was beautiful;
And that to me she seem'd to be all Nature,
And all varieties of things in one:
Would set at night in clouds of tears, and rise
All light and laughter in the morning; fear
No petty customs nor appearances;
But think what others only dream'd about;
And say what others did but think; and do
What others dared not do: so pure withal
In soul; in heart and act such conscious yet
Such perfect innocence, she made round her
A halo of delight. 'Twas these which won me;—
And that she never school'd within her breast
One thought or feeling, but gave holiday
To all; and that she made all even mine
In the communion of love: and we
Grew like each other, for we loved each other;
She, mild and generous as the air in spring;
And I, like earth all budding out with love.

Philip James Bailey (1816-1902)

Nuptial Sleep

At length their long kiss severed, with sweet smart:
And as the last slow sudden drops are shed
From sparkling eaves when all the storm has fled,
So singly flagged the pulses of each heart.
Their bosoms sundered, with the opening start
Of married flowers to either side outspread
From the knit stem; yet still their mouths, burnt red,
Fawned on each other where they lay apart.

Sleep sank them lower than the tide of dreams,
And their dreams watched them sink, and slid away.
Slowly their souls swam up again, through gleams
Of watered light and dull drowned waifs of day;
Till from some wonder of new woods and streams
He woke, and wondered more: for there she lay.

Dante Gabriel Rossetti (1828-1882)

It's All I Have to Bring Today

It's all I have to bring today--
This, and my heart beside--
This, and my heart, and all the fields--
And all the meadows wide--
Be sure you count--should I forget
Some one the sum could tell--
This, and my heart, and all the Bees
Which in the Clover dwell.

Emily Dickinson (1830-1886)

It's Such a Little Thing

It's such a little thing to weep,
So short a thing to sigh;
And yet by trades the size of these
We men and women die!

Emily Dickinson (1830-1886)

Love Is Enough

Love is enough: though the World be a-waning,
And the woods have no voice but the voice of complaining,
Though the sky be too dark for dim eyes to discover
The gold-cups and daisies fair blooming thereunder,
Though the hills be held shadows, and the sea a dark wonder,
And this day draw a veil over all deeds pass'd over,
Yet their hands shall not tremble, their feet shall not falter;
The void shall not weary, the fear shall not alter
These lips and these eyes of the loved and the lover.

William Morris (1834-1896)

Love Unexpressed

The sweetest notes among the human heart-strings are dull with rust;
The sweetest chords, adjusted by the angels, are clogged with dust;
We pipe and pipe again our dreary music upon the self-same strains,
While sounds of crime, and fear, and desolation, come back in sad refrains.

On through the world we go, an army marching with listening ears,
Each longing, sighing, for the heavenly music he never hears;
Each longing, sighing, for a word of comfort, a word of tender praise,
A word of love, to cheer the endless journey of earth's hard, busy days.

They love us, and we know it; this suffices for reason's share.
Why should they pause to give that love expression with gentle care?
Why should they pause? But still our hearts are aching with all the gnawing pain
Of hungry love that longs to hear the music, and longs and longs in vain.

We love them, and they know it; if we falter, with fingers numb,
Among the unused strings of love's expression, the notes are dumb.
We shrink within ourselves in voiceless sorrow, leaving the words unsaid,
And, side by side with those we love the dearest, in silence on we tread.

Thus on we tread, and thus each heart in silence its fate fulfils,
Waiting and hoping for the heavenly music beyond the distant hills.
The only difference of the love in heaven from love on earth below Is:
Here we love and know not how to tell it, and there we all shall know.

Constance Fenimore Woolson (1840-1894)

A Song of Love

Hey, rose, just born
Twin to a thorn;
Was't so with you, O Love and Scorn?

Sweet eyes that smiled,
Now wet and wild:
O Eye and Tear- mother and child.

Well: Love and Pain
Be kinfolks twain;
Yet would, Oh would I could Love again.

Sidney Lanier (1842-1881)

In the Garden VI: A Peach

If any sense in mortal dust remains
When mine has been refin'd from flower to flower,
Won from the sun all colours, drunk the shower
And delicate winy dews, and gain'd the gains
Which elves who sleep in airy bells, a-swing
Through half a summer day, for love bestow,
Then in some warm old garden let me grow
To such a perfect, lush, ambrosian thing
As this. Upon a southward-facing wall
I bask, and feel my juices dimly fed
And mellowing, while my bloom comes golden grey:
Keep the wasps from me! But before I fall
Pluck me, white fingers, and o'er two ripe-red
Girl lips O let me richly swoon away!

Edward Dowden (1843-1913)

Season of Love

When Spring in sunny woodland lay,
And gilded buds were sparely set
On oak tree and the thorny may,
I gave my love a violet.
"O Love," she said, and kissed my mouth
With one light, tender maiden kiss,
"There are no rich blooms in the south
So fair to me as this!"

When Summer reared her haughty crest,
We paused beneath the ruddy stars;
I placed a rose upon her breast,
Plucked from the modest casement bars.
"O Love," she said, and kissed my mouth--
Heart, heart, rememb'rest thou the bliss?--
"In east or west, in north or south,
I know no rose but this!"

When Autumn raised the purple fruit
In clusters to his bearded lips,
I laid a heartsease on the lute
That sang beneath her finger-tips.
"O Love," she said--and fair her eyes
Smiled thro' the dusk upon the lea--
"No heartsease glows beneath the skies
But this thou givest me!"

When Winter wept at shaking doors,
And holly trimmed his ermine vest,
And wild winds maddened on the moors,
I laid a flower upon her breast.
"Dear Heart," I whispered to the clay,
Which stilly smiled yet answered not,
"Bear thou to Heaven itself away
True love's Forget-me-not!"

Isabella Valancy Crawford (1850-1887)

Love In a Dairy

Of all the spots for making love,
Give me a shady dairy,
With crimson tiles, and blushing smiles
From its presiding fairy;
The jolly sunbeams peeping in
Thro' vine leaves all a-flutter,
Like greetings sent from Phoebus to
The Goddess of Fresh Butter.

The swallows twittering in the eaves,
The air of Summer blowing
Thro' open door from where a score
Of tall rose-trees are growing,
A distant file of hollyhocks,
A rugged bush of tansy,
And nearer yet beside the steps
A gorgeous purple pansy;

Suggestive scents of new-mown hay,
From lowland meadows coming;
The distant ripple of a stream,
And drowsy sounds of humming
From able-bodied bees that bevy
About the morning-glory,
Or dawdle pleasantly around
The apple-blossoms hoary.

A rosy bloom pervades the spot;
And where the shadows darkle,
In glittering rows the shining pans
Show many a brilliant sparkle.
As snowy as my lady's throat,
Or classic marble urn,
In central floor there proudly stands
The scourèd white-wood churn.

And she who reigns o'er churn and pan--
In truth, my friend, between us,
My dimpled Chloe is more fair

Than Milo's famous Venus.
Mark, mark those eyes so arch and dark,
Those lips like crimson clover,
And ask yourself, as well you may,
How I could prove a rover.

Talk not to me of moonlit groves,
Of empress, belle, or fairy;
To me the fairest love of loves
Is Chloe of the Dairy.

Isabella Valancy Crawford (1850-1887)

Late Loved--Well Loved

He stood beside her in the dawn--
And she his Dawn and she his Spring.
From her bright palm she fed her fawn,
Her swift eyes chased the swallow's wing;
Her restless lips, smile-haunted, cast
Shrill silver calls to hound and dove;
Her young locks wove them with the blast.
To the flushed azure shrine above
The light boughs o'er her golden head
Tossed emerald arm and blossom palm;
The perfume of their prayer was spread
On the sweet wind in breath of balm.

"Dawn of my heart," he said, "O child,
Knit they pure eyes a space with mine:
O crystal child eyes, undefiled,
Let fair love leap from mine to thine!"
"The Dawn is young," she, smiling, said,
"Too young for Love's dear joy and woe;
Too young to crown her careless head
With his ripe roses. Let me go
Unquestioned for a longer space;
Perchance when day is at the flood
In thy true palm I'll gladly place
Love's flower in its rounding bud.
But now the day is all too young,
The Dawn and I are playmates still."
She slipped the blossomed boughs among,
He strode beyond the violet hill.

Again they stand--Imperial Noon
Lays her red sceptre on the earth--
Where golden hangings make a gloom,
And far-off lutes sing dreamy mirth.
The peacocks cry to lily cloud
From the white gloss of balustrade;
Tall urns of gold the gloom make proud;
Tall statues whitely strike the shade
And pulse in the dim quivering light

Until, most Galatea-wise,
Each looks from base of malachite
With mystic life in limbs and eyes.

Her robe--a golden wave that rose,
And burst, and clung as water clings
To her long curves--about her flows.
Each jewel on her white breast sings
Its silent song of sun and fire.
No wheeling swallows smite the skies
And upward draw the faint desire,
Weaving its mystery in her eyes.
In the white kisses of the lips
Of her long fingers lies a rose:
Snow-pale beside her curving lips,
Red by her snowy breast it glows.

"Noon of my soul," said he, "behold
The day is ripe, the rose full blown!
Love stands in panoply of gold,
To Jovian height and strength now grown;
No infant he--a king he stands,
And pleads with thee for love again!"
"Ah, yes!" she said, "in all known lands
He kings it--lord of subtlest pain!
The moon is full, the rose of fair--
Too fair! 'tis neither white nor red!
I know the rose that love should wear
Must redden as the heart hath bled!
The moon is mellow bright, and I
Am happy in its perfect glow.
The slanting sun the rose may dye,
But for the sweet noon--let me go."

She parted--shimmering thro' the shade,
Bent the fair splendour of her head.
"Would the rich noon were past," he said;
"Would the pale rose were flushed to red!"

Again. The noon is past and Night
Binds on his brow the blood-red Mars;
Down dusky vineyards dies the fight,
And blazing hamlets slay the stars.
Shriek the shrill shells; the heated throats

Of thundrous cannon burst; and high
Scales the fierce joy of bugle notes
The flame-dimmed splendours of the sky.
He, dying, lies beside his blade,
Clear smiling as a warrior blest
With victory smiles; thro' sinister shade
Gleams the White Cross upon her breast.

"Soul of my soul, or is it night
Or is it dawn, or is it day?
I see no more nor dark nor light,
I hear no more the distant fray."
"'Tis Dawn," she whispers, "Dawn at last,
Bright flushed with love's immortal glow.
For me as thee all earth is past!
Late loved--well loved--now let us go!"

Isabella Valancy Crawford (1850-1887)

The Rose in the Deeps of his Heart

All things uncomely and broken,
all things worn-out and old,
The cry of a child by the roadway,
the creak of a lumbering cart,
The heavy steps of the ploughman,
splashing the wintry mould,
Are wronging your image that blossoms
a rose in the deeps of my heart.
The wrong of unshapely things
is a wrong too great to be told,
I hunger to build them anew
and sit on a green knoll apart,
With the earth and the sky and the water,
remade, like a casket of gold
For my dreams of your image that blossoms
a rose in the deeps of my heart.

William Butler Yeats (1865-1939)

The Sorrow of Love

The quarrel of the sparrows in the eaves,
The full round moon and the star-laden sky,
And the loud song of the ever-singing leaves,
Had hid away earth's old and weary cry.

And then you came with those red mournful lips,
And with you came the whole of the world's tears,
And all the sorrows of her labouring ships,
And all the burden of her myriad years.

And now the sparrows warring in the eaves,
The curd-pale moon, the white stars in the sky,
And the loud chaunting of the unquiet leaves
Are shaken with earth's old and weary cry.

William Butler Yeats (1865-1939)

William and Emily

There is something about Death
Like love itself!
If with some one with whom you have known passion,
And the glow of youthful love,
You also, after years of life
Together, feel the sinking of the fire,
And thus fade away together,
Gradually, faintly, delicately,
As it were in each other's arms,
Passing from the familiar room --
That is a power of unison between souls
Like love itself!

Edgar Lee Masters (1868-1950)

Retort

Thou art a fool," said my head to my heart,
"Indeed, the greatest of fools thou art,
To be led astray by trick of a tress,
By a smiling face or a ribbon smart;"
And my heart was in sore distress.

Then Phyllis came by, and her face was fair,
The light gleamed soft on her raven hair;
And her lips were blooming a rosy red.
Then my heart spoke out with a right bold air:
"Thou art worse than a fool, O head!"

Paul Laurence Dunbar (1872-1906)

If

If life were but a dream, my Love,
And death the waking time;
If day had not a beam, my Love,
And night had not a rhyme, --
A barren, barren world were this
Without one saving gleam;
I'd only ask that with a kiss
You'd wake me from the dream.

If dreaming were the sum of days,
And loving were the bane;
If battling for a wreath of bays
Could soothe a heart in pain, --
I'd scorn the meed of battle's might,
All other aims above
I'd choose the human's higher right,
To suffer and to love!

Paul Laurence Dunbar (1872-1906)

Passion and Love

A Maiden wept and, as a comforter,
Came one who cried, "I love thee,"
and he seized
Her in his arms and kissed her with hot breath,
That dried the tears upon her flaming cheeks.
While evermore his boldly blazing eye
Burned into hers; but she uncomforted
Shrank from his arms and only wept the more.

Then one came and gazed mutely in her face
With wide and wistful eyes; but still aloof
He held himself; as with a reverent fear,
As one who knows some sacred presence nigh.
And as she wept he mingled tear with tear,
That cheered her soul like dew a dusty flower,
Until she smiled, approached, and touched his
hand!

Paul Laurence Dunbar (1872-1906)

Venus Transiens

Tell me,
Was Venus more beautiful
Than you are,
When she topped
The crinkled waves,
Drifting shoreward
On her plaited shell?
Was Botticelli's vision
Fairer than mine;
And were the painted rosebuds
He tossed his lady
Of better worth
Than the words I blow about you
To cover your too great loveliness
As with a gauze
Of misted silver?

For me,
You stand poised
In the blue and buoyant air,
Cinctured by bright winds,
Treading the sunlight.
And the waves which precede you
Ripple and stir
The sands at my feet.

Amy Lowell (1874-1925)

The Taxi

When I go away from you
The world beats dead
Like a slackened drum.
I call out for you against the jutted stars
And shout into the ridges of the wind.
Streets coming fast,
One after the other,
Wedge you away from me,
And the lamps of the city prick my eyes
So that I can no longer see your face.
Why should I leave you,
To wound myself upon the sharp edges of the night?

Amy Lowell (1874-1925)

I Am Not Yours

I am not yours, not lost in you,
Not lost, although I long to be
Lost as a candle lit at noon,
Lost as a snowflake in the sea.

You love me, and I find you still
A spirit beautiful and bright,
Yet I am I, who long to be
Lost as a light is lost in light.

Oh plunge me deep in love, put out
My senses, leave me deaf and blind,
Swept by the tempest of your love,
A taper in a rushing wind.

Sara Teasdale (1884-1933)

Love and Death

Shall we, too, rise forgetful from our sleep,
And shall my soul that lies within your hand
Remember nothing, as the blowing sand
Forgets the palm where long blue shadows creep
When winds along the darkened desert sweep?

Or would it still remember, tho' it spanned
A thousand heavens, while the planets fanned
The vacant ether with their voices deep?
Soul of my soul, no word shall be forgot,
Nor yet alone, beloved, shall we see

The desolation of extinguished suns,
Nor fear the void wherethro' our planet runs,
For still together shall we go and not
Fare forth alone to front eternity.

Sara Teasdale (1884-1933)

Love-Free

I am free of love as a bird flying south in the autumn,
Swift and intent, asking no joy from another,
Glad to forget all of the passion of April
Ere it was love-free.

I am free of love, and I listen to music lightly,
But if he returned, if he should look at me deeply,
I should awake, I should awake and remember
I am my lover's.

Sara Teasdale (1884-1933)

Kindliness

When love has changed to kindliness—
Oh, love, our hungry lips, that press
So tight that Time's an old gold's dream
Nodding in heaven, and whisper stuff
Seven million years were not enough
To think on after, make it seem
Less than the breath of children playing,
A blasphemy scarce worth the saying,
A sorry jest, "When love has grown
To kindliness—to kindliness!" ...
And yet—the best that either's known
Will change, and wither, and be less,
At last, than comfort, or its own
Remembrance. And when some caress
Tendered in habit (once a flame
All heaven sang out to) wakes the shame
Unworded, in the steady eyes
We'll have,—that day, what shall we do?
Being so noble, kill the two
Who've reached their second-best? Being wise,
Break cleanly off, and get away.
Follow down other windier skies
New lures, alone? Or shall we stay,
Since this is all we've known, content
In the lean twilight of such day,
And not remember, not lament?
That time when all is over, and
Hand never flinches, brushing hand;
And blood lies quiet, for all you're near;
And it's but spoken words we hear,
Where trumpets sang; when the mere skies
Are stranger and nobler than your eyes;
And flesh is flesh, was flame before;
And infinite hungers leap no more
In the chance swaying of your dress;
And love has changed to kindliness.

Rupert Brooke (1887-1915)

The Dream

Love, if I weep it will not matter,
And if you laugh I shall not care;
Foolish am I to think about it,
But it is good to feel you there.
Love, in my sleep I dreamed of waking, --
White and awful the moonlight reached
Over the floor, and somewhere, somewhere,
There was a shutter loose, -- it screeched!
Swung in the wind, -- and no wind blowing! --
I was afraid, and turned to you,
Put out my hand to you for comfort, --
And you were gone! Cold, cold as dew,
Under my hand the moonlight lay!
Love, if you laugh I shall not care,
But if I weep it will not matter, --
Ah, it is good to feel you there!

Edna St. Vincent Millay (1892-1950)

Poet to His Love

An old silver church in a forest
Is my love for you.
The trees around it
Are words that I have stolen from your heart.
An old silver bell, the last smile you gave,
Hangs at the top of my church.
It rings only when you come through the forest
And stand beside it.
And then, it has no need for ringing,
For your voice takes its place.

Maxwell Bodenheim (1892-1954)

Poems About Love of Life

Daffodils

I wander'd lonely as a cloud
That floats on high o'er vales and hills,
When all at once I saw a crowd,
A host, of golden daffodils;
Beside the lake, beneath the trees,
Fluttering and dancing in the breeze.

Continuous as the stars that shine
And twinkle on the Milky Way,
They stretch'd in never-ending line
Along the margin of a bay;
Ten thousand saw I at a glance,
Tossing their heads in sprightly dance.

The waves beside them danced, but they
Out-did the sparkling waves in glee;
A poet could not but be gay,
In such a jocund company:
I gazed—and gazed—but little thought
What wealth the show to me had brought:

For oft, when on my couch I lie
In vacant or in pensive mood,
They flash upon that inward eye
Which is the bliss of solitude;
And then my heart with pleasure fills,
And dances with the daffodils.

William Wordsworth (1770-1850)

To a Butterfly

I've watched you now a full half-hour,
Self-poised upon that yellow flower;
And, little Butterfly! indeed
I know not if you sleep or feed.
How motionless!—not frozen seas
More motionless! and then
What joy awaits you, when the breeze
Hath found you out among the trees,
And calls you forth again!

This plot of orchard-ground is ours;
My trees they are, my Sister's flowers;
Here rest your wings when they are weary;
Here lodge as in a sanctuary!
Come often to us, fear no wrong;
Sit near us on the bough!
We'll talk of sunshine and of song,
And summer days, when we were young;
Sweet childish days, that were as long
As twenty days are now.

William Wordsworth (1770-1850)

Life Is Love

The fair varieties of earth,
The heavens serene and blue above,
The rippling smile of mighty seas—
What is the charm of all, but love?

By love they minister to thought,
Love makes them breathe the poet's song;
When their Creator best is prais'd,
'Tis love inspires the adoring throng.

Knowledge, and power, and will supreme,
Are but celestial tyranny,
Till they are consecrate by love,
The essence of divinity.

For love is strength, and faith, and hope;
It crowns with bliss our mortal state;
And, glancing far beyond the grave,
Foresees a life of endless date.

That life is love; and all of life
Time or eternity can prove;
Both men and angels, worms and gods
Exist in universal love.

William Johnson Fox (1786-1864)

from I Sing the Body Electric

1
I sing the body electric,
The armies of those I love engirth me and I engirth them,
They will not let me off till I go with them, respond to them,
And discorrupt them, and charge them full with the charge of the soul.

Was it doubted that those who corrupt their own bodies conceal themselves?
And if those who defile the living are as bad as they who defile the dead?
And if the body does not do fully as much as the soul? And if the body
were not the soul, what is the soul?

2
The love of the body of man or woman balks account, the body itself
balks account,
That of the male is perfect, and that of the female is perfect.

The expression of the face balks account,
But the expression of a well-made man appears not only in his face,
It is in his limbs and joints also, it is curiously in the joints of
his hips and wrists,
It is in his walk, the carriage of his neck, the flex of his waist
and knees, dress does not hide him,
The strong sweet quality he has strikes through the cotton and broadcloth,
To see him pass conveys as much as the best poem, perhaps more,
You linger to see his back, and the back of his neck and shoulder-side.

The sprawl and fulness of babes, the bosoms and heads of women, the
folds of their dress, their style as we pass in the street, the
contour of their shape downwards,
The swimmer naked in the swimming-bath, seen as he swims through
the transparent green-shine, or lies with his face up and rolls
silently to and from the heave of the water,
The bending forward and backward of rowers in row-boats, the
horse-man in his saddle,
Girls, mothers, house-keepers, in all their performances,
The group of laborers seated at noon-time with their open
dinner-kettles, and their wives waiting,
The female soothing a child, the farmer's daughter in the garden or
cow-yard,

The young fellow hosing corn, the sleigh-driver driving his six
horses through the crowd,
The wrestle of wrestlers, two apprentice-boys, quite grown, lusty,
good-natured, native-born, out on the vacant lot at sundown
after work,
The coats and caps thrown down, the embrace of love and resistance,
The upper-hold and under-hold, the hair rumpled over and blinding the eyes;
The march of firemen in their own costumes, the play of masculine
muscle through clean-setting trowsers and waist-straps,
The slow return from the fire, the pause when the bell strikes
suddenly again, and the listening on the alert,
The natural, perfect, varied attitudes, the bent head, the curv'd
neck and the counting;
Such-like I love- I loosen myself, pass freely, am at the mother's
breast with the little child,
Swim with the swimmers, wrestle with wrestlers, march in line with
the firemen, and pause, listen, count.

Walt Whitman (1819-1892)

Departure

Adieu, kind Life, though thou hast often been
Lavish of quip, and scant of courtesy,
Beneath thy roughness I have found in thee
A host who doth my parting favor win.
Friend, teacher, sage, and sometimes harlequin,
Thine every mood hath held some good for me,—
Nor even friendlier seemed thy company
Than on this night when I must quit thine inn.
I love thee, Life, in spite of thy rude ways!
Dear is thy pleasant house, so long my home.
I thank thee for the hospitable days,
The friends, the rugged cheer. Then, landlord, come!
Pour me a stirrup cup,—our parting nears:
I ever liked thy wine, though salt with tears.

May Riley Smith (1842-1927)

A New Hymn for Solitude

I found Thee in my heart, O Lord,
As in some secret shrine;
I knelt, I waited for Thy word,
I joyed to name Thee mine.

I feared to give myself away
To that or this; beside
Thy altar on my face I lay,
And in strong need I cried.

Those hours are past. Thou art not mine,
And therefore I rejoice,
I wait within no holy shrine,
I faint not for the voice.

In Thee we live; and every wind
Of heaven is Thine; blown free
To west, to east, the God unshrined
Is still discovering me.

Edward Dowden (1843-1913)

Life

A crust of bread and a corner to sleep in,
A minute to smile and an hour to weep in,
A pint of joy to a peck of trouble,
And never a laugh but the moans come double;
And that is life!

A crust and a corner that love makes precious,
With a smile to warm and the tears to refresh us;
And joy seems sweeter when cares come after,
And a moan is the finest of foils for laughter;
And that is life!

Paul Laurence Dunbar (1872-1906)

Under the Harvest Moon

Under the harvest moon,
When the soft silver
Drips shimmering
Over garden nights,
Death, the gray mocker,
Comes and whispers to you
As a beautiful friend
Who remembers.

Under the summer roses
When the flagrant crimson
Lurks in the dusk
Of the wild red leaves,
Love, with little hands,
Comes and touches you
With a thousand memories,
And asks you
Beautiful, unanswerable questions.

Carl Sandburg (1878-1967)

Poems About Losing Love

Love Me Little, Love Me Long

Love me little, love me long,
Is the burden of my song.
Love that is too hot and strong
Burneth soon to waste.
Still, I would not have thee cold,
Not too backward, nor too bold;
Love that lasteth till 'tis old
Fadeth not in haste.
Love me little, love me long,
Is the burden of my song.

If thou lovest me too much,
It will not prove as true as touch;
Love me little, more than such,
For I fear the end.
I am with little well content,
And a little from thee sent
Is enough, with true intent
To be steadfast friend.
Love me little, love me long,
Is the burden of my song.

Say thou lov'st me while thou live;
I to thee my love will give,
Never dreaming to deceive
Whiles that life endures.
Nay, and after death, in sooth,
I to thee will keep my truth,
As now, when in my May of youth;
This my love assures.
Love me little, love me long,
Is the burden of my song.

Constant love is moderate ever,
And it will through life persever;
Give me that, with true endeavor
I will it restore.

A suit of durance let it be,
For all weathers that for me,
For the land or for the sea,
Lasting evermore.
*Love me little, love me long,
Is the burden of my song.*

Winter's cold, or summer's heat,
Autumn's tempests on it beat,
It can never know defeat,
Never can rebel.
Such the love that I would gain,
Such the love, I tell thee plain,
Thou must give, or woo in vain;
So to thee, farewell!
*Love me little, love me long,
Is the burden of my song.*

Anonymous (1500-1600)

A Summer Song

When as the rye reach to the chin,
And chopcherry, chopcherry ripe within,
Strawberries swimming in the cream,
And school-boys playing in the stream;
Then O, then O, then O my true love said,
Till that time come again,
She could not live a maid.

George Peele (1558-1598)

Farewell to Love

Since there's not help, come let us kiss and part;
Nay, I am done, you get no more of me;
And I am glad, yea, glad with all my heart,
That thus so cleanly I myself can free;
Shake hands for ever, cancel all our vows,
And when we meet at any time again,
Be it not seen in either of our brows
That we, one jot of former love retain.
Now, at the last gasp of love's latest breath,
When his pulse failing, passion speechless lies,
When faith is kneeling by his bed of death,
And innocence is closing up his eyes,
Now, if thou wouldst, when all have given him over,
From death to life Thou mightst him yet recover.

Michael Drayton (1563-1631)

Sonnet 73

That time of year thou mayst in me behold
When yellow leaves, or none, or few, do hang
Upon those boughs which shake against the cold,
Bare ruin'd choirs, where late the sweet birds sang.
In me thou see'st the twilight of such day
As after sunset fadeth in the west;
Which by and by black night doth take away,
Death's second self, that seals up all in rest.
In me thou see'st the glowing of such fire,
That on the ashes of his youth doth lie,
As the death-bed, whereon it must expire,
Consum'd with that which it was nourish'd by.
This thou perceiv'st, which makes thy love more strong,
To love that well, which thou must leave ere long.

William Shakespeare (1564-1616)

Still to be Neat

Still to be neat, still to be drest,
As you were going to a feast;
Still to be powder'd, still perfum'd:
Lady, it is to be presum'd,
Though art's hid causes are not found,
All is not sweet, all is not sound.

Give me a look, give me a face,
That make simplicity a grace;
Robes loosely flowing, hair as free:
Such sweet neglect more taketh me
Than all th'adulteries of art.
They strike mine eyes, but not my heart.

Ben Jonson (1572-1637)

The Hour-Glass

Consider this small dust, here in the glass,
By atoms moved:
Could you believe that this the body was
Of one that loved;
And in his mistress' flame playing like a fly,
Was turned to cinders by her eye:
Yes ; and in death, as life unblest,
To have't exprest,
Even ashes of lovers find no rest.

Ben Jonson (1572-1637)

Song: Sweetest love I do not go . . .

Sweetest love, I do not go,
For weariness of thee,
Nor in hope the world can show
A fitter love for me;
But since that I
Must die at last, 'tis best
To use myself in jest
Thus by feign'd deaths to die.

Yesternight the sun went hence,
And yet is here today;
He hath no desire nor sense,
Nor half so short a way:
Then fear not me,
But believe that I shall make
Speedier journeys, since I take
More wings and spurs than he.

O how feeble is man's power,
That if good fortune fall,
Cannot add another hour,
Nor a lost hour recall!
But come bad chance,
And we join to it our strength,
And we teach it art and length,
Itself o'er us to advance.

When thou sigh'st, thou sigh'st not wind,
But sigh'st my soul away;
When thou weep'st, unkindly kind,
My life's blood doth decay.
It cannot be
That thou lov'st me, as thou say'st,
If in thine my life thou waste,
That art the best of me.

Let not thy divining heart
Forethink me any ill;
Destiny may take thy part,

And may thy fears fulfil;
But think that we
Are but turn'd aside to sleep;
They who one another keep
Alive, ne'er parted be.

John Donne (1572-1631)

I Loved a Lass

I Loved a lass, a fair one,
As fair as e'er was seen;
She was indeed a rare one,
Another Sheba Queen:
But, fool as then I was,
I thought she loved me too:
But now, alas! she's left me,
Falero, lero, loo!

Her hair like gold did glister,
Each eye was like a star,
She did surpass her sister,
Which pass'd all others far;
She would me 'honey' call,
She'd--O she'd kiss me too!
But now, alas! she's left me,
Falero, lero, loo!

In summer time to Medley
My love and I would go;
The boatmen there stood read'ly
My love and me to row.
For cream there would we call,
For cakes and for prunes too;
But now, alas! she's left me,
Falero, lero, loo!

Her cheeks were like the cherry,
Her skin was white as snow;
When she was blithe and merry
She angel-like did show;
Her waist exceeding small,
The fives did fit her shoe:
But now, alas! she's left me,
Falero, lero, loo!

In summer time or winter
She had her heart's desire;
I still did scorn to stint her

From sugar, sack, or fire;
The world went round about,
No cares we ever knew:
But now, alas! she's left me,
Falero, lero, loo!

To maidens' vows and swearing
Henceforth no credit give;
You may give them the hearing,
But never them believe;
They are as false as fair,
Unconstant, frail, untrue:
For mine, alas! hath left me,
Falero, lero, loo!

George Wither (1588-1667)

Song

For her gait if she be walking,
Be she sitting I desire her
For her state's sake, and admire her
For her wit if she be talking:
Gait and state and wit approve her;
For which all and each I love her.

Be she sullen, I commend her
For a modest; be she merry,
For a kind one her prefer I.
Briefly, everything doth lend her
So much grace and so approve her
That for everything I love her.

William Browne (1591-1643)

To the Willow-tree

Thou art to all lost love the best,
The only true plant found,
Wherewith young men and maids distrest,
And left of love, are crown'd.

When once the lover's rose is dead,
Or laid aside forlorn:
Then willow-garlands 'bout the head
Bedew'd with tears are worn.

When with neglect, the lovers' bane,
Poor maids rewarded be
For their love lost, their only gain
Is but a wreath from thee.

And underneath thy cooling shade,
When weary of the light,
The love-spent youth and love-sick maid
Come to weep out the night.

Robert Herrick (1591-1674)

The Constant Lover

Out upon it, I have loved
Three whole days together!
And am like to love three more,
If it prove fair weather.

Time shall moult away his wings
Ere he shall discover
In the whole wide world again
Such a constant lover.

But the spite on 't is, no praise
Is due at all to me:
Love with me had made no stays,
Had it any been but she.

Had it any been but she,
And that very face,
There had been at least ere this
A dozen dozen in her place.

Sir John Suckling (1609-1642)

Love Armed

Love in Fantastique Triumph satt,
Whilst bleeding Hearts around him flow'd,
For whom Fresh pains he did create,
And strange Tryanic power he show'd;
From thy Bright Eyes he took his fire,
Which round about, in sport he hurl'd;
But 'twas from mine he took desire,
Enough to undo the Amorous World.
From me he took his sighs and tears,
From thee his Pride and Crueltie;
From me his Languishments and Feares,
And every Killing Dart from thee;
Thus thou and I, the God have arm'd,
And sett him up a Deity;
But my poor Heart alone is harm'd,
Whilst thine the Victor is, and free.

Aphra Behn (1640-1689)

Upon the Death of Her Husband

Yet, gentle shade! whether thou now does rove,
Thro' some blest vale, or ever verdant grove,
One moment listen to my grief and take
The softest vows that ever love can make.
For thee, all thoughts of pleasure I forgo,
For Thee, my tears shall never cease to flow;
For thee at once I from the world retire,
To feed in silent shades a hopeless fire.
My bosom all thy image shall retain,
The full impression there shall still remain
As thou has taught my tender heart to prove
The noblest height and elegance of love,
That sacred passion I to thee confine.
My spotless faith shall be for ever thine.

Elizabeth Singer Rowe (1674-1737)

Love's Secret

Never seek to tell thy love,
Love that never told can be;
For the gentle wind doth move
Silently, invisibly.

I told my love, I told my love,
I told her all my heart,
Trembling, cold, in ghastly fears,
Ah! she did depart!

Soon after she was gone from me
A traveller came by,
Silently, invisibly,
He took her with a sigh.

William Blake (1757-1827)

My Pretty Rose Tree

A flower was offered to me,
Such a flower as May never bore;
But I said "I've a pretty rose tree,"
And I passed the sweet flower o'er.

Then I went to my pretty rose tree,
To tend her by day and by night;
But my rose turned away with jealousy,
And her thorns were my only delight.

William Blake (1757-1827)

A Red, Red Rose

O my Luve's like a red, red rose
That's newly sprung in June:
O my Luve's like the melodie
That's sweetly play'd in tune!

As fair thou art, my bonnie lass,
So deep in love am I:
And I will love thee still, my dear,
Till a' the seas gang dry:

Till a' the seas gang dry, my dear,
And the rocks melt with the sun;
I will luve thee still my dear,
When the sands of life shall run.

And fare thee weel, my only Luve,
And fare thee weel a while!
And I will come again, my Luve,
Tho' it were ten thousand mile.

Robert Burns (1759-1796)

The Banks of Bonnie Doon

Ye flowery banks o' bonnie Doon,
How can ye blume sae fair!
How can ye chant, ye little birds,
And I sae fu' o' care!
Thou'll break my heart, thou bonnie bird
That sings upon the bough;
Thou minds me o' the happy days
When my fause* Luve was true.
Thou'll break my heart, thou bonnie bird
That sings beside thy mate;
For sae I sat, and sae I sang,
And wist na o' my fate.
Aft hae I roved by bonnie Doon
To see the woodbine twine,
And ilka* bird sang o' its love;
And sae did I o' mine.
Wi' lightsome heart I pu'd a rose,
Frae aff its thorny tree;
And my fause luver staw* the rose,
But left the thorn wi' me.

Robert Burns (1759-1796)

She Dwelt Among Untrodden Ways

She dwelt among the untrodden ways
Beside the springs of Dove,
Maid whom there were none to praise
And very few to love:

A violet by a mosy tone
Half hidden from the eye!
---Fair as a star, when only one
Is shining in the sky.

She lived unknown, and few could know
When Lucy ceased to be;
But she is in her grave, and, oh,
The difference to me!

William Wordsworth (1770-1850)

Surprised by Joy - Impatient as the Wind

Surprised by joy — impatient as the Wind
I turned to share the transport--Oh! with whom
But Thee, deep buried in the silent tomb,
That spot which no vicissitude can find?
Love, faithful love, recalled thee to my mind--
But how could I forget thee? Through what power,
Even for the least division of an hour,
Have I been so beguiled as to be blind
To my most grievous loss?--That thought's return
Was the worst pang that sorrow ever bore,
Save one, one only, when I stood forlorn,
Knowing my heart's best treasure was no more;
That neither present time, nor years unborn
Could to my sight that heavenly face restore.

William Wordsworth (1770-1850)

Love Lies Bleeding

You call it, Love lies bleeding--so you may,
Though the red Flower, not prostrate, only droops,
As we have seen it here from day to day,
From month to month, life passing not away:
A flower how rich in sadness! Even thus stoops,
(Sentient by Grecian sculpture's marvellous power)
Thus leans, with hanging brow and body bent
Earthward in uncomplaining languishment
The dying Gladiator. So, sad Flower!
('T is Fancy guides me willing to be led,
Though by a slender thread,)
So drooped Adonis bathed in sanguine dew
Of his death-wound, when he from innocent air
The gentlest breath of resignation drew;
While Venus in a passion of despair
Rent, weeping over him, her golden hair
Spangled with drops of that celestial shower.
She suffered, as Immortals sometimes do;
But pangs more lasting far, that Lover knew
Who first, weighed down by scorn, in some lone bower
Did press this semblance of unpitied smart
Into the service of his constant heart,
His own dejection, downcast Flower! could share
With thine, and gave the mournful name which thou wilt ever bear.

William Wordsworth (1770-1850)

Desideria

Surprised by joy, impatient as the Wind
I turned to share the transport O! with whom
But Thee, deep buried in the silent tomb,
That spot which no vicissitude can find?
Love, faithful love, recall'd thee to my mind
But how could I forget thee? Through what power,
Even for the least division of an hour,
Have I been so beguiled as to be blind
To my most grievous loss? That thought's return
Was the worst pang that sorrow ever bore,
Save one, one only, when I stood forlorn,
Knowing my heart's best treasure was no more;
That neither present time, nor years unborn
Could to my sight that heavenly face restore.

William Wordsworth (1770-1850)

At the Mid Hour of Night

At the mid hour of night, when stars are weeping, I fly
To the lone vale we loved, when life shone warm in thine eye;
And I think oft, if spirits can steal from the regions of air,
To revisit past scenes of delight, thou wilt come to me there,
And tell me our love is remember'd, even in the sky.

Then I sing the wild song 'twas once such pleasure to hear!
When our voices commingling breathed, like one, on the ear;
And, as Echo far off through the vale my said orison rolls,
I think, oh my love! 'tis thy voice from the Kingdom of Souls,
Faintly answering still the notes that once were so dear.

Thomas Moore (1779-1852)

So We'll Go No More a Roving

So, we'll go no more a roving
So late into the night,
Though the heart be still as loving,
And the moon be still as bright.
For the sword outwears its sheath,
And the soul wears out the breast,
And the heart must pause to breathe,
And love itself have rest.
Though the night was made for loving,
And the day returns too soon,
Yet we'll go no more a roving
By the light of the moon.

Lord George Gordon Byron (1788-1824)

When We Two Parted

When we two parted
In silence and tears,
Half broken-hearted,
To sever for years,
Pale grew thy cheek and cold,
Colder thy kiss;
Truly that hour foretold
Sorrow to this.

The dew of the morning
Sank chill on my brow
It felt like the warning
Of what I feel now.
Thy vows are all broken,
And light is thy fame:
I hear thy name spoken,
And share in its shame.

They name thee before me,
A knell to mine ear;
A shudder comes o'er me
Why wert thou so dear?
They know not I knew thee,
Who knew thee too well:
Long, long shall I rue thee
Too deeply to tell.

In secret we met
In silence I grieve
That thy heart could forget,
Thy spirit deceive.
If I should meet thee
After long years,
How should I greet thee?
With silence and tears.

Lord George Gordon Byron (1788-1824)

To ———

Music, when soft voices die,
Vibrates in the memory.—
Odours, when sweet violets sicken,
Live within the sense they quicken.—

Rose leaves, when the rose is dead,
Are heap'd for the beloved's bed—
And so thy thoughts, when thou art gone,
Love itself shall slumber on.

Percy Bysshe Shelley (1792-1822)

When the Lamp is Shattered

When the lamp is shattered
The light in the dust lies dead -
When the cloud is scattered,
The rainbow's glory is shed.
When the lute is broken,
Sweet tones are remembered not;
When the lips have spoken,
Loved accents are soon forgot.
As music and splendour
Survive not the lamp and the lute,
The heart's echoes render
No song when the spirit is mute -
No song but sad dirges,
Like the wind through a ruined cell,
Or the mournful surges
That ring the dead seaman's knell.
When hearts have once mingled,
Love first leaves the well-built nest;
The weak one is singled
To endure what it once possessed.
O Love! who bewailest
The frailty of all things here,
Why choose you the frailest
For your cradle, your home, and your bier?
Its passions will rock thee,
As the storms rock the ravens on high;
Bright reason will mock thee,
Like the sun from a wintry sky.
From thy nest every rafter
Will rot, and thine eagle home
Leave thee naked to laughter,
When leaves fall and cold winds come.

Percy Bysshe Shelley (1792-1822)

Music, When Soft Voices Die

Music, when soft voices die,
Vibrates in the memory—
Odours, when sweet violets sicken,
Live within the sense they quicken.

Rose leaves, when the rose is dead,
Are heap'd for the beloved's bed;
And so thy thoughts when thou are gone,
Love itself shall slumber on.

Percy Bysshe Shelley (1792-1822)

Why is the Rose so Pale

Ah Dearest, canst thou tell me why
The Rose should be so pale?
And why the azure Violet
Should wither in the vale?
And why the Lark should, in the cloud,
So sorrowfully sing?
And why from loveliest balsam-buds
A scent of death should spring?
And why the Sun upon the mead
So chillingly should frown?
And why the Earth should, like a grave,
Be mouldering and brown?
And why is it that I, myself,
So languishing should be?
And why is it, my Heart-of-Hearts,
That thou forsakest me?

Heinrich Heine (1797-1856)

A Dream within a Dream

Take this kiss upon the brow!
And, in parting from you now,
Thus much let me avow:
You are not wrong who deem
That my days have been a dream;
Yet if hope has flown away
In a night, or in a day,
In a vision, or in none,
Is it therefore the less gone?
All that we see or seem
Is but a dream within a dream.

I stand amid the roar
Of a surf-tormented shore,
And I hold within my hand
Grains of the golden sand--
How few! yet how they creep
Through my fingers to the deep,
While I weep--while I weep!
O God! can I not grasp
Them with a tighter clasp?
O God! can I not save
One from the pitiless wave?
Is *all* that we see or seem
But a dream within a dream?

Edgar Allan Poe (1809-1849)

Annabel Lee

It was many and many a year ago,
In a kingdom by the sea,
That a maiden there lived whom you may know
By the name of Annabel Lee;
And this maiden she lived with no other thought
Than to love and be loved by me.

I was a child and she was a child,
In this kingdom by the sea:
But we loved with a love that was more than love -
I and my Annabel Lee;
With a love that the winged seraphs of heaven
Coveted her and me.

And this was the reason that, long ago,
In this kingdom by the sea,
A wind blew out of a cloud, chilling
My beautiful Annabel Lee;
So that her high-born kinsmen came
And bore her away from me,
To shut her up in a sepulchre
In this kingdom by the sea.

The angels, not half so happy in heaven,
Went envying her and me -
Yes! that was the reason (as all men know,
In this kingdom by the sea)
That the wind came out of the cloud one night,
Chilling and killing my Annabel Lee.

But our love it was stronger by far than the love
Of those who were older than we -
Of many far wiser than we -
And neither the angels in heaven above,
Nor the demons down under the sea,
Can ever dissever my soul from the soul
Of the beautiful Annabel Lee;

For the moon never beams without bringing me dreams

Of the beautiful Annabel Lee;
And the stars never rise but I feel the bright eyes
Of the beautiful Annabel Lee;
And so, all the night-tide, I lie down by the side
Of my darling -my darling -my life and my bride,
In the sepulchre there by the sea -
In her tomb by the sounding sea.

Edgar Allan Poe (1809-1849)

To One in Paradise

Thou wast all that to me, love,
For which my soul did pine-
A green isle in the sea, love,
A fountain and a shrine,
All wreathed with fairy fruits and flowers,
And all the flowers were mine.

Ah, dream too bright to last!
Ah, starry Hope! that didst arise
But to be overcast!
A voice from out the Future cries,
"On! on!"- but o'er the Past
(Dim gulf!) my spirit hovering lies
Mute, motionless, aghast!

For, alas! alas! me
The light of Life is o'er!
"No more- no more- no more-"
(Such language holds the solemn sea
To the sands upon the shore)
Shall bloom the thunder-blasted tree
Or the stricken eagle soar!

And all my days are trances,
And all my nightly dreams
Are where thy grey eye glances,
And where thy footstep gleams-
In what ethereal dances,
By what eternal streams.

Edgar Allan Poe (1809-1849)

I Leave Thee for Awhile

I leave thee for awhile, my love, I leave thee with a sigh;
The fountain spring within my soul is playing in mine eye;
I do not blush to own the tear, let, let it touch my cheek,
And what my lip has failed to tell, that drop perchance may speak.
Mavourneen! when again I seek my green isle in the West,
Oh, promise thou wilt share my lot, and set this heart at rest.

I leave thee for awhile, my love; but every hour will be
Uncheered and lonely till the one that brings me back to thee.
I go to make my riches more; but where is man to find
A vein of gold so rich and pure as that I leave behind?
Mavourneen! though my home might be the fairest earth possessed,
Till thou wouldst share and make it warm, this heart would know no rest.

I leave thee for awhile, my love; my cheek is cold and white,
But ah, I see a promise stand within thy glance of light;
When next I seek old, Erin's shore, thy step will bless it too,
And then the grass will seem more green, the sky will have more blue.
Mavourneen! first and dearest loved, there's sunshine in my breast,
For thou wilt share my future lot, and set this heart at rest.

Eliza Cook (1818-1889)

Remembrance

Cold in the earth—and the deep snow piled above thee,
Far, far removed, cold in the dreary grave!
Have I forgot, my only Love, to love thee,
Sever'd at last by Time's all-severing wave?

Now, when alone, do my thoughts no longer hover
Over the mountains, on that northern shore,
Resting their wings where heath and fern-leaves cover
Thy noble heart for ever, ever more?

Cold in the earth—and fifteen wild Decembers
From those brown hills have melted into spring:
Faithful, indeed, is the spirit that remembers
After such years of change and suffering!

Sweet Love of youth, forgive, if I forget thee,
While the world's tide is bearing me along;
Other desires and other hopes beset me,
Hopes which obscure, but cannot do thee wrong!

No later light has lighten'd up my heaven,
No second morn has ever shone for me;
All my life's bliss from thy dear life was given,
All my life's bliss is in the grave with thee.

But when the days of golden dreams had perish'd,
And even Despair was powerless to destroy;
Then did I learn how existence could be cherish'd,
Strengthen'd and fed without the aid of joy.

Then did I check the tears of useless passion—
Wean'd my young soul from yearning after thine;
Sternly denied its burning wish to hasten
Down to that tomb already more than mine.

And, even yet, I dare not let it languish,
Dare not indulge in memory's rapturous pain;
Once drinking deep of that divinest anguish,
How could I seek the empty world again?

Emily Bronte (1818-1848)

A Farewell

With all my will, but much against my heart,
We two now part.
My Very Dear,
Our solace is, the sad road lies so clear.
It needs no art,
With faint, averted feet
And many a tear,
In our opposèd paths to persevere.
Go thou to East, I West.
We will not say
There 's any hope, it is so far away.
But, O, my Best,
When the one darling of our widowhead,
The nursling Grief,
Is dead,
And no dews blur our eyes
To see the peach-bloom come in evening skies,
Perchance we may,
Where now this night is day,
And even through faith of still averted feet,
Making full circle of our banishment,
Amazèd meet;
The bitter journey to the bourne so sweet
Seasoning the termless feast of our content
With tears of recognition never dry.

Coventry Patmore (1823-1896)

Severed Selves

Two separate divided silences,
Which, brought together, would find loving voice;
Two glances which together would rejoice
In love, now lost like stars beyond dark trees;
Two hands apart whose touch alone gives ease;
Two bosoms which, heart-shrined with mutual flame,
Would, meeting in one clasp, be made the same;
Two souls, the shores wave-mocked of sundering seas:--

Such are we now. Ah! may our hope forecast
Indeed one hour again, when on this stream
Of darkened love once more the light shall gleam?
An hour how slow to come, how quickly past,
Which blooms and fades, and only leaves at last,
Faint as shed flowers, the attenuated dream.

Dante Gabriel Rossetti (1828-1882)

If You Were Coming in the Fall

If you were coming in the fall,
I'd brush the summer by
With half a smile and half a spurn,
As housewives do a fly.

If I could see you in a year,
I'd wind the months in balls,
And put them each in separate drawers,
Until their time befalls.

If only centuries delayed,
I'd count them on my hand,
Subtracting till my fingers dropped
Into Van Diemen's land.

If certain, when this life was out,
That yours and mine should be,
I'd toss it yonder like a rind,
And taste eternity.

But now, all ignorant of the length
Of time's uncertain wing,
It goads me, like the goblin bee,
That will not state its sting.

Emily Dickinson (1830-1886)

For Each Ecstatic Instant

For each ecstatic instant
We must an anguish pay
In keen and quivering ratio
To the ecstasy.

For each beloved hour
Sharp pittances of years,
Bitter contested farthings
And coffers heaped with tears.

Emily Dickinson (1830-1886)

I Lost a World

I lost a World - the other day!
Has Anybody found?
You'll know it by the Row of Stars
Around its forehead bound.

A Rich man—might not notice it—
Yet—to my frugal Eye,
Of more Esteem than Ducats—
Oh find it—Sir—for me!

Emily Dickinson (1830-1886)

You Left Me, Sweet, Two Legacies

You left me, sweet, two legacies,--
A legacy of love
A Heavenly Father would content,
Had He the offer of;

You left me boundaries of pain
Capacious as the sea,
Between eternity and time,
Your consciousness and me.

Emily Dickinson (1830-1886)

Remember

Remember me when I am gone away,
Gone far away into the silent land;
When you can no more hold me by the hand,
Nor I half turn to go yet turning stay.
Remember me when no more day by day
You tell me of our future that you plann'd:
Only remember me; you understand
It will be late to counsel then or pray.
Yet if you should forget me for a while
And afterwards remember, do not grieve:
For if the darkness and corruption leave
A vestige of the thoughts that once I had,
Better by far you should forget and smile
Than that you should remember and be sad.

Christina Georgina Rossetti (1830-1894)

Echo

Come to me in the silence of the night;
Come in the speaking silence of a dream;
Come with soft rounded cheeks and eyes as bright
As sunlight on a stream;
Come back in tears,
O memory of hope, love of finished years.

O dream how sweet, too sweet, too bitter-sweet,
Whose wakening should have been in Paradise,
Where souls brim-full of love abide and meet;
Where thirsting longing eyes
Watch the slow door
That opening, letting in, lets out no more.

Yet come to me in dreams, that I may live
My very life again though cold in death;
Come back to me in dreams, that I may give
Pulse for pulse, breath for breath:
Speak low, lean low,
As long ago, my love, how long ago.

Christina Georgina Rossetti (1830-1894)

To an Absent Lover

That so much change should come when thou dost go,
Is mystery that I cannot ravel quite.
The very house seems dark as when the light
Of lamps goes out. Each wonted thing doth grow
So altered, that I wander to and fro
Bewildered by the most familiar sight,
And feel like one who rouses in the night
From dream of ecstasy, and cannot know
At first if he be sleeping or awake.
My foolish heart so foolish for thy sake
Hath grown, dear one!
Teach me to be more wise.
I blush for all my foolishness doth lack;
I fear to seem a coward in thine eyes.
Teach me, dear one,—but first thou must come back!

Helen Hunt Jackson (1830-1885)

Heart, We Will Forget Him!

Heart, we will forget him!
You an I, tonight!
You may forget the warmth he gave,
I will forget the light.

When you have done, pray tell me
That I my thoughts may dim;
Haste! lest while you're lagging,
I may remember him!

Emily Dickinson (1830-1886)

Proud of My Broken Heart

Proud of my broken heart since thou didst break it,
Proud of the pain I did not feel till thee,
Proud of my night since thou with moons dost slake it,
Not to partake thy passion, my humility.

Emily Dickinson (1830-1886)

To Lose Thee

To lose thee, sweeter than to gain
All other hearts I knew.
'Tis true the drought is destitute
But, then, I had the dew!
The Caspian has its realms of sand,
Its other realm of sea.
Without this sterile perquisite
No Caspian could be.

Emily Dickinson (1830-1886)

The Going

Why did you give no hint that night
That quickly after the morrow's dawn,
And calmly, as if indifferent quite,
You would close your term here, up and be gone
Where I could not follow
With wing of swallow
To gain one glimpse of you ever anon!

Never to bid good-bye
Or lip me the softest call,
Or utter a wish for a word, while I
Saw morning harden upon the wall,
Unmoved, unknowing
That your great going
Had place that moment, and altered all.

Why do you make me leave the house
And think for a breath it is you I see
At the end of the alley of bending boughs
Where so often at dusk you used to be;
Till in darkening dankness
The yawning blankness
Of the perspective sickens me!

You were she who abode
By those red-veined rocks far West,
You were the swan-necked one who rode
Along the beetling Beeny Crest,
And, reining nigh me,
Would muse and eye me,
While Life unrolled us its very best.

Why, then, latterly did we not speak,
Did we not think of those days long dead,
And ere your vanishing strive to seek
That time's renewal? We might have said,
"In this bright spring weather
We'll visit together
Those places that once we visited."

Well, well! All's past amend,
Unchangeable. It must go.
I seem but a dead man held on end
To sink down soon. . . . O you could not know
That such swift fleeing
No soul foreseeing -
Not even I - would undo me so!

Thomas Hardy (1840-1928)

I Have Loved Flowers That Fade

I have loved flowers that fade,
  Within whose magic tents
Rich hues have marriage made
  With sweet unmemoried scents:
    A honeymoon delight—
    A joy of love at sight,
    That ages in an hour—
    My song be like a flower!

I have loved airs that die
  Before their charm is writ
    Along a liquid sky
    Trembling to welcome it.
  Notes, that with pulse of fire
  Proclaim the spirit's desire,
  Then die, and are nowhere—
    My song be like an air!

Die, song, die like a breath,
  And wither as a bloom;
Fear not a flowery death,
  Dread not an airy tomb!
  Fly with delight, fly hence!
'Twas thine love's tender sense
  To feast; now on thy bier
  Beauty shall shed a tear.

Robert Bridges (1844-1930)

The Night Has a Thousand Eyes

The night has a thousand eyes,
And the day but one;
Yet the light of the bright world dies
With the dying sun.

The mind has a thousand eyes,
And the heart but one;
Yet the light of a whole life dies
When love is done.

Francis William Bourdillon (1852-1921)

When I Was One-and-Twenty

When I was one-and-twenty
I heard a wise man say,
'Give crowns and pounds and guineas
But not your heart away;
Give pearls away and rubies
But keep your fancy free.'
But I was one-and-twenty,
No use to talk to me.

When I was one-and-twenty
I heard him say again,
'The heart out of the bosom
Was never given in vain;
'Tis paid with sighs a plenty
And sold for endless rue.'
And I am two-and-twenty,
And oh, 'tis true, 'tis true.

A. E. Housman (1859-1936)

When You Are Old

When you are old and grey and full of sleep,
And nodding by the fire, take down this book,
And slowly read, and dream of the soft look
Your eyes had once, and of their shadows deep;

How many loved your moments of glad grace,
And loved your beauty with love false or true,
But one man loved the pilgrim soul in you,
And loved the sorrows of your changing face;

And bending down beside the glowing bars,
Murmur, a little sadly, how Love fled
And paced upon the mountains overhead
And hid his face amid a crowd of stars.

William Butler Yeats (1865-1939)

Reluctance

Out through the fields and the woods
And over the walls I have wended;
I have climbed the hills of view
And looked at the world, and descended;
I have come by the highway home,
And lo, it is ended.

The leaves are all dead on the ground,
Save those that the oak is keeping
To ravel them one by one
And let them go scraping and creeping
Out over the crusted snow,
When others are sleeping.

And the dead leaves lie huddled and still,
No longer blown hither and thither;
The last long aster is gone;
The flowers of the witch-hazel wither;
The heart is still aching to seek,
But the feet question 'Whither?'

Ah, when to the heart of man
Was it ever less than a treason
To go with the drift of things,
To yield with a grace to reason,
And bow and accept the end
Of a love or a season?

Robert Frost (1874-1963)

May

The wind is tossing the lilacs,
The new leaves laugh in the sun,
And the petals fall on the orchard wall,
But for me the spring is done.

Beneath the apple blossoms
I go a wintry way,
For love that smiled in April
Is false to me in May.

Sara Teasdale (1884-1933)

I Thought of You

I thought of you and how you love this beauty,
And walking up the long beach all alone
I heard the waves breaking in measured thunder
As you and I once heard their monotone.

Around me were the echoing dunes, beyond me
The cold and sparkling silver of the sea,
We two will pass through death and ages lengthen
Before you hear that sound again with me.

Sara Teasdale (1884-1933)

The Kiss

I hoped that he would love me,
And he has kissed my mouth,
But I am like a stricken bird
That cannot reach the south.

For though I know he loves me,
To-night my heart is sad;
His kiss was not so wonderful
As all the dreams I had.

Sara Teasdale (1884-1933)

Elegy

Since I lost you, my darling, the sky has come near,
And I am of it, the small sharp stars are quite near,
The white moon going among them like a white bird among snow-berries,
And the sound of her gently rustling in heaven like a bird I hear.

And I am willing to come to you now, my dear,
As a pigeon lets itself off from a cathedral dome
To be lost in the haze of the sky, I would like to come,
And be lost out of sight with you, and be gone like foam.

For I am tired, my dear, and if I could lift my feet,
My tenacious feet from off the dome of the earth
To fall like a breath within the breathing wind
Where you are lost, what rest, my love, what rest!

D.H. Lawrence (1885-1930)

Love

Love is a breach in the walls, a broken gate,
Where that comes in that shall not go again;
Love sells the proud heart's citadel to Fate.
They have known shame, who love unloved. Even then,
When two mouths, thirsty each for each, find slaking,
And agony's forgot, and hushed the crying
Of credulous hearts, in heaven—such are but taking
Their own poor dreams within their arms, and lying
Each in his lonely night, each with a ghost.
Some share that night. But they know love grows colder,
Grows false and dull, that was sweet lies at most.
Astonishment is no more in hand or shoulder,
But darkens, and dies out from kiss to kiss.
All this is love; and love is but this.

Rupert Brooke (1887-1915)

Ebb

I know what my heart is like
Since your love died:
It is like a hollow ledge
Holding a little pool
Left there by the tide,
A little tepid pool,
Drying inward from the edge.

Edna St. Vincent Millay (1892-1950)

Poems About Love and Friendship

A Book of Verse

A book of verse, underneath the bough,
A jug of wine, a loaf of bread - and thou
Beside me singing in the wilderness -
Ah, wilderness were paradise now!

Omar Khayyam (1048-1131)

Sonnet CIV

To me, fair friend, you never can be old
For as you were when first your eye I ey'd,
Such seems your beauty still. Three winters cold
Have from the forests shook three summers' pride,
Three beauteous springs to yellow autumn turn'd
In process of the seasons I have seen,
Three April perfumes in three hot Junes burn'd,
Since first I saw you fresh, which yet are green.
Ah! yet doth beauty, like a dial-hand,
Steal from this figure, and no pace perceiv'd;
So your sweet hue, which methinks still doth stand,
Hath motion, and mine eye may be deceiv'd:
For fear of which, hear this, thou age unbred:
Ere you were born was beauty's summer dead.

William Shakespeare (1564-1616)

Friendship

When we were idlers with the loitering rills,
The need of human love we little noted:
Our love was nature; and the peace that floated
On the white mist, and dwelt upon the hills,
To sweet accord subdued our wayward wills:
One soul was ours, one mind, one heart devoted,
That, wisely doting, ask'd not why it doted,
And ours the unknown joy, which knowing kills.
But now I find how dear thou wert to me;
That man is more than half of nature's treasure,
Of that fair beauty which no eye can see,
Of that sweet music which no ear can measure;
And now the streams may sing for others' pleasure,
The hills sleep on in their eternity.

Hartley Coleridge (1796-1849)

We Have Been Friends Together

We have been friends together,
In sunshine and in shade;
Since first beneath the chestnut-trees
In infancy we played.
But coldness dwells within thy heart,
A cloud is on thy brow;
We have been friends together—
Shall a light word part us now?

We have been gay together;
We have laugh'd at little jests;
For the fount of hope was gushing
Warm and joyous in our breasts.
But laughter now hath fled thy lip,
And sullen glooms thy brow;
We have been gay together—
Shall a light word part us now?

We have been sad together,
We have wept, with bitter tears,
O'er the grass-grown graves, where slumber'd
The hopes of early years.
The voices which are silent there
Would bid thee clear thy brow;
We have been sad together—
Oh! what shall part us now?

Caroline Elizabeth Sarah Norton (1808-1877)

Love and Friendship

Love is like the wild rose-briar,
Friendship like the holly-tree -
The holly is dark when the rose-briar blooms'
But which will bloom most constantly?

The wild rose-briar is sweet in spring,
It's summer blossoms scent the air.
Yet wait tlll winter comes again
And who will call the wild-briar fair?

Then scorn the silly rose-wreath now
And deck thee with the holly's sheen,
That when December blights thy brow
He still may leave thy garland green.

Emily Bronte (1818-1848)

Last

Friend, whose smile has come to be
Very precious unto me,
Though I know I drank not first
Of your love's bright fountain-burst,
Yet I grieve not for the past,
So you only love me last!

Other souls may find their joy
In the blind love of a boy:
Give me that which years have tried,
Disciplined and purified,—
Such as, braving sun and blast,
You will bring to me at last!

There are brows more fair than mine,
Eyes of more bewitching shine,
Other hearts more fit, in truth,
For the passion of your youth;
But, their transient empire past,
You will surely love me last!

Wing away your summer-time,
Find a love in every clime,
Roam in liberty and light,—
I shall never stay your flight,
For I know, when all is past
You will come to me at last!

Elizabeth Akers Allen (1832-1867)

To F.J.S.

I read, dear friend, in your dear face
Your life's tale told with perfect grace;
The river of your life, I trace
Up the sun-chequered, devious bed
To the far-distant fountain-head.

Not one quick beat of your warm heart,
Nor thought that came to you apart,
Pleasure nor pity, love nor pain
Nor sorrow, has gone by in vain;

But as some lone, wood-wandering child
Brings home with him at evening mild
The thorns and flowers of all the wild,
From your whole life, O fair and true
Your flowers and thorns you bring with you!

Robert Louis Stevenson (1850-1894)

Harlan Sewall

You never understood, O unknown one,
Why it was I repaid
Your devoted friendship and delicate ministrations
First with diminished thanks,
Afterward by gradually withdrawing my presence from you,
So that I might not be compelled to thank you,
And then with silence which followed upon
Our final Separation.
You had cured my diseased soul. But to cure it
You saw my disease, you knew my secret,
And that is why I fled from you.
For though when our bodies rise from pain
We kiss forever the watchful hands
That gave us wormwood, while we shudder
For thinking of the wormwood,
A soul that's cured is a different matter,
For there we'd blot from memory
The soft-toned words, the searching eyes,
And stand forever oblivious,
Not so much of the sorrow itself
As of the hand that healed it.

Edgar Lee Masters (1868-1950)

O, My Friend

O, my friend,
What fitting word can I say?
You, my chum,
My companion of infinite talks,
My inspiration,
My guide,
Through whom I saw myself at best;
You, the light of this western country.
You, a great richness.
A glory,
A charm,
Product and treasure of these States.

Bill, I knew you had gone.
I was walking down into town this morning,
And amid the hurry of cars and the flash of this July sun,
You came to me.
At least the intimation came to me;
And may it be you,
That somewhere I can laugh and talk long hours with you again.

Edgar Lee Masters (1868-1950)

A Time to Talk

When a friend calls to me from the road
And slows his horse to a meaning walk,
I don't stand still and look around
On all the hills I haven't hoed,
And shout from where I am, What is it?
No, not as there is a time to talk.
I thrust my hoe in the mellow ground,
Blade-end up and five feet tall,
And plod: I go up to the stone wall
For a friendly visit.

Robert Frost (1874-1963)

14672927R00155

Made in the USA
San Bernardino, CA
01 September 2014